KIDS' PRANKS and CAPERS

RECOLLECTIONS OF A MISSPENT YOUTH

by

Frank Reed

Illustrations by
Bridget Heriz-Smith

TOFTWOOD • DEREHAM • NORFOLK

Published by:
NOSTALGIA PUBLICATIONS
(Terry Davy)
7 Elm Park, Toftwood,
Dereham, Norfolk
NR19 1NB

First impression: October 1998

© Frank Reed

ISBN 0 947630 22 8

Design and typesetting:
NOSTALGIA PUBLICATIONS

Printed by:
PAGE BROS. (NORWICH) LTD.
Mile Cross Lane,
Norwich,
Norfolk NR6 6SA

Dedication

For Tim, Jon, Ben and Charlie, who have heard them all many times.

Contents

Introduction

The purpose of this book is to record for posterity some of the adventures of a gang of boys in North Suffolk, in the years before the Second World War. From their activities a picture of life during those hard times may be seen. While the illustrations are often imaginative, they also convey and comment on the spirit of the times. It is clear that cold houses, poor clothing and lack of money, were small barriers to a full, interesting and happy childhood. Another hazard was the attitude of many adults, who were as likely as not to clip your ears or buffet your head, but the lines were well drawn and you knew where you stood. You kept out of the way and did your best to avoid detection. Not being caught was a matter of great pride.

The members of the gang were not particularly well behaved, except as a front to deceive adults, but neither were they notable for villainy. A failure to join in the sort of activities recounted would have achieved a label of 'goody goody', or 'cissy', resulting in expulsion from the company of your peers. But when the grown ups showed that they did try to understand, a great deal of co-operation could be obtained from the children.

It is comforting to look back on those days as a type of blue sky 'golden age'. In summer the sun always shone, at least during school holidays. Skating and sledging were possible every winter, nobody caused trouble and toddlers took great joy in the seven times table. Perhaps the activities of the gang will remind us that children could be as much of a nuisance then as now.

I would like to thank my old school friend, David Woodward, and Terry Davy, a new friend, for their encouragement and help, also to express my gratitude to Bridget Heriz-Smith, who brought skill and imagination to the illustrations, as well as inexhaustible patience.

Frank Reed
Onehouse, Stowmarket
October 1998

Mind Your Head

Do you ever sit in a public auditorium where things can be dropped on you from the balcony? You would not do this if you had my childhood experience.

In the years before the second war the Regent cinema ran a Saturday morning show known as the 'tuppenny shove', because it cost two pennies (nearly 1p) to get in via the disorderly queue. People called the Regent 'The Fleapit' or 'The Itchpit', but if it was infested we remained free of vermin.

Others said that ferrets and rats were taken in and released, but who would want to lose a valuable ferret? Nor did any rats appear on our frequent visits, though the thought of the chaos that would follow was tempting, and if rats had been readily available no doubt it would have been tried.

The film often broke down, leading to shouts and choruses of 'Why are we waiting?' At such times apple cores and other assorted missiles were thrown at the screen and the female ushers ran for cover, pleading with the projectionist to stop the chaos by quick repairs. But it was not until I had threepence for the balcony that I realised the true and terrible nature of the prevailing disorder.

Flash Gordon had just completed, until next week, his usual competent destruction of the wicked aliens who had been foolish enough to attack Earth. Unfortunately their leader, Ming the Merciless, ruler of the universe, had again escaped, returning to his home planet, Mongo. It was then that I became aware that every piece of rubbish was thrown over the edge. I had heard that young men took cherries into the cinema and squeezed the pips between their fingers to bombard the audience. We could not afford such exotic items, but now, skins and cores, sweet wrappings and spent chewing gum seemed to provoke small complaint from the unfortunates in the tuppennies below, but the girl next to me was intent on real damage. It was a bit much and I looked at Roy. He shook his head and whispered, 'She's thirteen. One of the Applecart gang's best fighters. Look at her shoulders.'

So we pretended to watch the screen while she unscrewed the metal supporting arm of her chair and threw it over. Even so, the lower classes did nothing more than shout abuse and promises of retribution. Presumably it had not hit anybody, or had landed upholstery side down. But for them, nemesis was on the way.

Buck Rogers came next, his task to finish off the few unfortunate space dwellers who had escaped Flash, but his enemies were the Red Mongols, and he blasted them in a hundred mythic battles fought across the immensities of space. Nobody seemed to realise that the same actor played both characters, and still less did they bother that they were seeing consecutive science fiction talkies.

The baddies were frequently cheered and the goodies booed because few children paid enough attention to know the difference. The great thing was to be there, crowded together in the semi-darkness, part of a rich, streetwise experience.

As the episode neared its end, with Buck captured again and about to meet his doom, a large girl of about twelve led a small boy down the side aisle, next to the wall. They walked along the solid front of the balcony until they reached the decorative ironwork grille in front of the central gangway. There they stopped while the little boy turned his back and spread his legs for a minute or two. His sister glared aggressively at anybody who gazed too hard, though most children did not notice, suddenly becoming interested in the mayhem wrought by the aliens' new death ray.

6

But this time the lower rabble did protest, especially when they found that the wet stuff was not water. Squeals and yells rose as they realised any one of them could have been deluged.

The picture stopped to the usual loud protests and hail of missiles, but this time it was no breakdown. The burly uniformed commissionaire stamped up to the balcony so we all knew it was serious. But no one would split, for the little boy's sister had a fearful reputation. It was she whom I had seen pinning down a boy, rifling his pockets for any vouchers he had collected. In one of the many intervals the commissionaire distributed these vouchers, three of which gave free entry to a future performance. He broadcast them from a basket, as if he was sowing seed, and utter disorder followed. Shouting children ran up and down the gangways, jumped over the seats, scratched and scrabbled, stole and fought. Some even tried to grab their share from the basket but merely bounced off the growling giant in the uniform. The only safe place for the small or weak was under the seat or near the entrance. Even then, some bully might trap your head or arm between the lifted seat and its back.

So nobody told on the Amazon, but I have never sat within range of the balcony since. Always, I have minded my head.

Free Smellie

The lovely red telephone box at the bottom of the road was free, if you knew how to work it. We had discovered this on one of our button B tours.

To make a call two pennies (nearly 1p) had to be put in the machine before you dialled the number. Then, when somebody answered, you pressed button B and the pennies clattered down, never to return. The person at the other end could not hear you until this happened. If there was no reply, you pressed button B and got your money back. It was amazing how many people forgot to press button B, and we spent a lot of

time doing it for them, though of course they were not present. We made about a shilling (5p) a week. The town was divided into spheres of influence, just as Al Capone split up Chicago, and we had two boxes on our side, the town gangs having the rest.

The great spin off from this activity was that we found the box at the bottom of our road required no money from us. To make a free call, we put in two pennies, the person answered and when the conversation ended we pressed button B and our money came back. The knowledge was not much use to us since nobody we knew was on the phone and ringing people just to make rude remarks soon palled. Then, oh joy, we discovered a Smellie listed. His life became hell, for we often rang to ask, 'Are you Smellie?' If he answered yes, we retorted, 'Well go and have a bath.'

Or, 'This is the perfume shop. Would you like some scent?'

Then we sat on the kerb outside the box and laughed ourselves silly. Our question to poor Smellie varied, as did the answer.

A lot of time was spent examining the directory in the post office for other useful names but our courage failed before we completed the task. The counter clerks began to ask why we spent so much time looking up numbers, so nobody else suffered. It was just as well because the phone people heard about it and there was a rumour that they were watching the box. After several months it was repaired and Smellie was free.

Another Day

'Look,' shouted Roy. 'A painter's scow. Against the rules to leave them on the Hamilton beach.'

'Yeah,' said Billy. 'Good chance for us, though. We could sail it round the harbour.'

Near the edge of the water was a craft about twelve feet long, pointed at one end and square at the other. Ancient and blackened wooden sides stood up vertically about a foot, and two thick seats gave it internal strength. It was splashed with colour in rainbow hues.

'Flat bottomed. Won't rock when the painters stand up, but weighs a ton. We'd never get it into the water. And what would Thirkettle say?'

'He never comes here,' said Billy. 'Come on. Let's start digging. The tide's coming in and that should help.'

So we began. Rubbish of all sorts littered the tide line and it was among the rotting tyres, dead bladderwrack and decaying crabs that we found the fish box. Roy broke it up quickly and without fuss, banging with a large pebble from behind the sea wall where he could not be seen. He put the nails in his pocket to straighten later and soon had several pieces of board to use as spades and paddles. With these we started to scoop sand from around the scow. It was dirty brown and stained our hands. Opaque wavelets lapped into the canals and caressed the sides of the small vessel, but there was no magic in them and it remained firmly stuck. The water was green and murky, streaked with tiny iridescent slicks of oil. It always seemed thicker than the sea, pounding the wall behind us, and rumour said that it would give you a rash if you swam in it.

'Concentrate on the stern,' said Billy. It was steady digging till the incoming tide gurgled louder against the woodwork. 'Now on the sides, nearest the water,' he added. 'Start to dig underneath.'

Hard work made little impression. With three of us pushing, the bulky craft would not move, but Billy was full of ideas.

'Get in the stern and jump,' he said. 'Then at the bows.'

At the fourth attempt the boat tipped slightly and waves splashed away from the square end. We jumped out and with a great deal of push and shove the scow crunched through the sand and slid gently into the harbour.

At first it was difficult to steer, but Billy used the biggest piece of the spade wood as a rudder and soon we were off. He looked round, expecting a shout from the fish quay but nothing happened. No pleasure craft were allowed in the dock, and even model boats were prohibited. He could imagine what Harbour Master Thirkettle would say and do if he found out.

It was pleasant in the middle of the harbour, with the sun hot on our faces and dancing diamonds on the waves. Relaxation came too soon.

'Listen,' said Arthur. 'That's Thirkettle's boat. What are we going to do, Billy?'

'Paddle round the other side of that trawler. Quick.'

We were puffed by the time we reached the shelter of the larger boat.

'Suppose he come this side,' wailed Arthur. 'I'm afeard.'

'Shut your tater trap and don't worry,' said Billy. 'He'll go the other side first and then come here.'

And so it happened. Thirkettle cruised past and as he turned to sail down our side of the trawler the scow eased round the bows and away from him.

'He looks puzzled,' said Roy. 'I bet somebody told him and he can't understand why nobody's here.'

'Go careful,' muttered Billy as we steered along the scored and blackened planks of the fishing boat. 'When he returns he'll be able to see us if he looks over his shoulder. We must get back to the other side.'

But it was too late. Attracted by a shout and pointing finger from the fish market, Thirkettle looked round and started to turn his motor boat.

'Pull for the shore boys. Paddle like hell,' yelled Billy.

'We'll never do it,' wailed Arthur.

'Yes we will,' said Billy. 'The harbour launch take a foot or more water while this thing'll go right up to the sand. He'll have to stop and get out, and he won't run very fast with his sea boots up to his thighs.'

Billy was right. Twenty feet from the shore Thirkettle's launch grounded heavily, throwing him off the seat, while we were out, splashing through a few inches of water. At the top of the sea wall we stopped and watched. He had sufficient sense to know he would never catch us, but waved his fist in the air.

'I'll have you yet,' he bawled. 'There'll be another day.'

That was something to think about. We knew he was right. Luck might not be on our side, another day.

The Next Election

'Vote, vote, vote for Mister Sorensen,
Kick old Loftus in the eye.
If Sorensen's the winner,
We'll have a Sunday dinner,
If we only kick old Loftus in the eye.'

'Sorensen in the teapot, Loftus in the spout,
Sorensen just blew his nose and shot old Loftus out.'

But he did not. The Reverend R. W. Sorensen, the Labour candidate, returned to his pulpit and Mr P. C. Loftus became Conservative Member of Parliament for the Suffolk (East) Lowestoft (451) constituency. He won 48% of the votes and had a majority of 1,920. He proved to be a good constituency MP, which Billy said meant Missing Person. Afterwards he won the favour of all, including many Labour voters, by saying, 'If Beccles were in Germany, everybody would say, you must see Beccles. But it isn't, thank God, so nobody comes.'

He was also reputed to accept the statement that Yarmouth was built on the mud that Beccles did not want, and that certainly did him no harm.

The ditties above were the theme songs of a group of youthful Labour supporters along with others too scurrilous to print. The Roadsters gang formed a primitive band comprised of anything that would make a noise, but also included attempts at instrumentation. There were comb and paper bazookas, bone clappers, pieces of rusty iron rod hit with another piece, galvanised dustbin lids and 'shakers', treacle tins filled with stones. Occasionally these were joined by a bugler whose best attempts reminded us of a dying cow. As well as marching and singing, the gang included in its activities alteration and defacement of posters, heckling outdoor speakers, and a little mild intimidation. The noise of the band approaching was enough to send many people into houses or shops.

But the action most enjoyed was election day attacks on Conservative cars. It made a change from assaults on vehicles from Norfolk conducted from Darby's timber yard, just before the bridge over the Waveney. Two or three days before voting began, Shash, the gang leader of the time, called Arthur, Roy and Billy together.

'Just make sure there's plenty of water around in case the earth's too hard,' he told them, and the three assembled a collection of old buckets and cans behind the hedge at the bottom of the hill, below the haunted heath. They filled them from the ditch.

When the day came, the conspirators met behind the hedge after school and began to roll the wet clods into balls. Soon the Conservative cars would appear, taking their supporters to vote. When a suitable target passed, the clods were thrown, and being good shot country boys able to bring down a bird, most scored direct hits. Wet clods were used since they would not damage the paintwork or break the mostly celluloid windows. There was a loony left school of thought which said that Tories deserved stones and damn the damage, but the centre held that this would bring the authorities out in force.

'Blue poster car, let 'em have it,' one of the boys at either end of the line would shout and bombardment began. It seems surprising now that the activity was tolerated, but what could the victims do? By the time a car had stopped, and the portly grown ups had scrambled out and found the gate, we were away, secure in the knowledge that most adults could run faster, but only for a hundred yards or so. Given a hundred and fifty yards start we were safe. Few of them would relish running over a muddy field in their best suits. They would know, too, that we had a palm-of-our-hand familiarity with the countryside, our regular marauding ground, and would easily outwit followers. There was a look out in the hedge on the other side of the meadow in case the adults got cunning and came round behind us. This office went to a very pressed smaller boy who was threatened with a beating if the job was not properly done. Shash told him, 'Think yourself lucky. If we're caught, you can say you were not with us.'

But we all knew that we would not be caught and that little Arny did not want to be watchman. He wanted to throw clods. Our only real fear was that Big Brian, one of the special constables, would appear, for he was a redoubtable runner, fast and enduring despite his size. As it turned out, he was needed at the polling booths, and on such a day, everybody was too busy to bother with the perennial nuisance of the gangs.

As the evening wore on, the number of targets reduced, partly because the cars had collected all those from village and hamlet who wished to vote, and partly because wise drivers learned to take another route rather than run the clod gauntlet. Boredom set in.

'Time we went home,' said Shash. He shouted across the road, 'We're going now. Mind you keep behind the hedge and we'll see you at the top.'

In the safety of the back gardens the two gangs compared notes.

'We got seventeen cars,' said Shash. 'Mostly the same ones. I got young Billy to take the numbers.'

'Only three for us,' moaned the Conservative gang. 'Labour don't have many cars. We'll join you, next election.'

Entry Free

'Got any money?' was the cry as Saturday approached. Often there was none, so how to get into the children's Saturday morning show at the Regent set a problem.

Between them the little gang managed to get hold of four halfpennies, so young Billy took them and bought one tuppeny ticket. Immediately on entry he called at the lavatory, waited till it was empty, and pushed quietly on the bar of the safety door. The alley was clear except for Roy and Arthur, oozing guilt as they slipped in. They rushed for the auditorium but Billy stopped them.

'Not all at once,' he cautioned. 'Somebody might notice. You go first, Arthur.'

Roy left next, then Billy. The much fingered half ticket nestled in his pocket, but he felt confident. The attendants used to check, and if they found you without a ticket it meant a swift and sometimes painful exit, especially if you struggled. Caught by the large man in the gaudy uniform, boys were likely to be thrown down the steps outside. But many parents found their peaceful morning disturbed by returning children, protesting that it was not fair. They had bought tickets and lost them, they said, and had been thrown out. So many Mums and Dads complained that the check ups stopped.

'Easy,' said Roy. It was, and the gang used this method even when they had money. They thought it would go on for ever, but soon learned a priceless lesson, to stay with them all their lives. All things, good and bad, come to an end. After a couple of months they were unlucky. The Applecart gang passed the alley entrance as Billy opened up. They rushed forward but were too late and had to be satisfied with nearly kicking the door down.

Billy knew they would be waiting outside the entrance afterwards.

'You let us in or we'll tell,' they threatened.

'Not all of you,' argued Billy, trying to salvage something from what he thought was a lost cause. 'They'll notice. Two of yours and two of ours next week and a different four the following week. We could keep it up for ever then.'

It was no good. Fred, their burly leader, ruled by brawn, not brain, and insisted all ten should be let in. Billy knew it was over.

'Tell you what. We've had a long run and we owe you for the time you misled the police for us. You have it.'

Roy grumbled.

'What did you want to do that for?'

'Work it out,' Billy replied. 'There's ten of them and three of us. Besides, how many weeks do you think it'll go on now? The Applecart lot are good fighters but they never work anything out.'

So the three paid their tuppences and watched developments. The first Saturday eight were in the alley, and when the door opened they rushed into the cinema. Their boasts about their success could be heard everywhere, so the next week about thirty were waiting. The exit from the lavatory into the auditorium was blocked with a noisy, struggling crowd and the commissionaire guessed immediately. There was a fearful row and the police were called.

'It wasn't our idea,' the Applecart gang complained, pointing. 'It was them. They did it first.'

But no adult ever believed anything any boy said, so Billy, Roy and Arthur were safe. All the same, they kept their mouths shut and tried to look innocent. Six months later it had all been forgotten and they had another successful run at the Regent, once more entry free.

Widdershins

'If you're going to do that I'm going home now,' said Billy. 'Suppose you did raise the devil, what would you do with him? Worse, what would he do with you?'

Roy told everybody that if you recited the Lord's Prayer backwards and ran round the church widdershins, that is, anti clockwise, it would raise the devil.

'We'd have to do it on Good Friday, then,' said Arthur. 'The devil can't hurt you then, and if you make the sign of the cross that's safe to say it backwards.'

'Don't believe there is a devil,' said Roy. 'That's just parson's talk, eh, Billy.'

'I'm not sure. Like I said, what would you do with him? Do you think you could put him in a bottle like the genie in Aladdin?'

'That's no worse than your brother. He put ink in the holy water in the church,' retorted Roy. 'My mother told me several people had black crosses on their faces. Then somebody noticed and they cleaned it out. And he keep on giving out leaflets and writing THWTP everywhere.'

'What's that mean?' asked Arthur.

'To Hell With The Pope,' Billy said. 'I told him he'd get into trouble. He's got religious mania. Anyway, what's he got to do with it? I'm going home. You can have the devil to yourselves.'

So the gang wandered home. The devil and widdershins would have to wait.

Funnel and Line

Steam enveloped the boys and nothing could be seen.

'Did it go in?' asked Roy.

'Don't know,' said Billy. 'Couldn't see. I'm covered in smuts and one went in my eye. If the stone did go in it hasn't done anything.'

The three coach train of the LNER, the London and North Eastern Railway that people called the Late Never Early Railway, cruised gently to a halt. Passengers from Yarmouth descended and the station staff were busy coupling on the carriages from Lowestoft. This was the only time to get up to mischief safely. The Station Master and his minions considered, with great justification, that boys, by nature, were bound to be up to no good and kept a strict watch except when trains were arriving and departing.

'Wait for the shunter,' said Roy. 'Won't be letting off steam.'

With many shouts of 'London train,' blowing of whistles and waving of green flags the engine prepared to depart. A last minute passenger was pushed in and the last door slammed. People waved. The spotless apple green locomotive puffed rythmic blasts of white steam into the air, everything shuddered, and she slowly pulled out.

'Coming,' said Roy. 'Make sure you're on target this time.'

Billy waited for the black 4-4-2 tank engine. It should be easy, for only a faint haze issued from the funnel. As it clanked nearer, Billy put his hand through the criss cross metal parapet, low down, and released the large pebble.

'I heard it hit something,' said Arthur. 'I'm afeard. Better stay low in case the boiler blow.'

Quite what the boys expected was hard to say. Certainly, if they had really thought an explosion would follow then no stones would ever have been dropped into the funnel. The tank reached the points and reversed off the main line. Eventually they learned from an engine driver friend that there was a grille in the funnel designed especially to prevent access to flying birds, or dropping stones.

Well away from the station and observation, above the London Road crossing, the little gang tried another trick.

'Only a small screw,' said Arthur. 'We don't want to derail it.'

'No chance,' said Billy. 'I asked my Dad and he said you shouldn't put anything on the line, but even a large screw couldn't affect a train.'

So a rusty two inch screw was set upright and the boys waited for the Eastern Belle, non-stop from Liverpool Street to Yarmouth.

'Due any minute now,' said Roy with his ear to the line. 'I can hear it.'

He would not have done this unless there was a lookout to tell him in case it came too soon. Nor would any of the little gang play 'last across.' Some boys claimed to lie down between the lines and let the train thunder over them, but few people believed it and nobody had ever seen them. The express whistled as it shot down the bank at a good seventy miles an hour, fair warning to anybody in the station of the hurricane about to sweep through. What happened to the screw was a mystery, for it was never found, and nor were any of the others that they put on the line.

'We could try a ha'penny,' suggested Arthur. 'Shash told me it got squashed till it was as big as a penny and he used one for sweets.'

'He's having you on,'said Billy. 'I'm not risking my Wednesday money.'

Arthur produced a halfpenny.

'Out of my Mum's purse,' he explained. 'She won't mind.'

This time it was a lumbering black monster pulling fifty two trucks and the halfpenny came out twice its normal size and very thin.

'Told you. It looks like a penny,' said Arthur as he picked it up. Billy laughed.

'You'll need a blind shopkeeper and even he'll think it's too thin. And the moment you try it on they'll know you've been putting things on the line and they might guess about the funnel.'

Timewatch

When I was eleven my grandmother gave me a watch. It proved one of the minor disasters of my early life.

We often journeyed into the countryside for the day. Sometimes we would take bread and jam sandwiches, (no butter or margarine) and a bottle of water, although if we were lucky this might be replaced with sharp tasting lemonade made from shop crystals. On such occasions we returned when we felt like it, which often meant missing a meal. The rule was that you could eat it if you were there and got nothing till the next if you were not. This did not bother us, but my grandmother thought meals should be regular, and that something should be done. Ever practical, she therefore bought me a watch.

It was a rather handsome affair, with Roman figures and a gun-metal case, part of which folded down to protect the glass. She thought it would be stronger than ordinary metal, a belief left over from the Great War. Anything made of the same material as the guns of the Western Front must be strong, she reasoned. The others were not impressed.

'Now they know we know the time they'll tell us when to come home,' said Roy. They thought only cissies from well off families possessed watches, and made their feelings known.

'Can't you just forget it?' asked Arthur. 'Last time we were late my mother said there was no excuse now we knew the time and sent me to bed without any tea.'

Nobody knew what to do, but like some problems left alone this one solved itself. On a sunny blue Saturday we walked to the family tree, so called because half a dozen kids could sit comfortably in its split trunk, fifteen feet off the ground. Another fork above us had always been a challenge and was the object of the expedition, so up we scrambled. And down I fell, making the amateur mistake of leaning on a rotten branch. Fortunately the lower foliage slowed my landing and the thick grass cushioned my collapse.

'You all right?' called Roy, laughing. 'Left your watch behind. I'll cop it down.'

'No, it might break.'

He laughed again and threw it down anyway. I picked it from the ground. The case was bent and a half inch branch had pushed through the face and into the works.

'Nobody's going to mend that,' chorused the others. 'Shan't have to bother with the time any more.'

And so it proved. Grandmother was very cross and told me I should look after my things.

'Money doesn't grow on trees,' she complained. I saw the funny side of that but thought it best not to smile.

'We'll see what your father says.'

I knew what his attitude would be.

'I can't stop the boy climbing trees. It's what boys do,' he said. 'Perhaps he should have left it at home.'

So we stopped watching the timepiece. I've never carried a watch since.

Spare the Rod

Johnny's Mum was not pleased when she found great crested newts in her washing. They were glorious, the flashiest creatures in the pond, and we caught them with nets, lures of tadpoles, and worms on strings. It was not babbing, where the worm was threaded through with twine. We did not like the idea of putting a needle through the worm in cold blood, and for the same reason never used fishhooks with barbs, or even bent pins. All this, despite the fact that a home made fishing rod was easy to craft from a piece of hedge nuttery, with a curtain ring attached to the end to loop thin kite string through. The real fisher boys among us added a float made from an old cork with a chicken feather on top.

We could not bear to cause physical hurt to newts. From above, the dark, greenish brown backs of the crested variety gave no hint of pleasures to come. Only as they were seen close to did the white speckles on the sides appear, and the bright orange or yellow, marbled with black spots, become visible underneath. A streak of bluish white on the side of the tail completed the rainbow display. The males bore ravishing, saw toothed crests, which distinguished them from the duller females. It was a permanent puzzle to us that in nature, the males were almost always the more attractive while in human beings it was the other way round.

Where to put our newts was a problem. Their four to six inch lengths meant that they were not happy in the two pound jam jars in which we brought them home, but it was the best way to see them. We put our noses to the jars and were full of wonder. I don't know what the newts thought but they did not seem unduly disturbed.

'In the water butt,' said Johnny. 'It'll be better for them than in the jar. More room.'

It was true. The Council supplied galvanised corrugated iron butts for its houses. They were about three feet deep and two feet in diameter, designed to give housewives some soft water. Johnny removed and hid the lid so the creatures would have some light.

'Your Mum gets water for washing clothes from there,' warned Billy.

'I'll take 'em out afore Monday,' he said. He was always the one for the quick fix and clear up the trouble afterwards.

Mrs Strowger was scrubbing a sheet. She used a board about three feet long and ten inches wide, the hard grain raised high by use. You could run your fingers along and imagine it as some sort of relief map of a rectangular island, where the mountains all ran the same way. Age and soap had given the board a yellowish cast.

It rested on the edge of a large, grey, galvanised bath with a handle at each end, while the rest of the board tilted into soapy cloudy six inch deep hot water. She spread her sheet over the board, soaped it with the tough bar of Sunlight and scrubbed the dirt away. It was hard labour. Occasionally she trooped outside to get a hand-cup of soft water from the rain water butt.

That was when the neighbours heard the scream. Rushing round to find the cause, they saw a hysterical woman tottering out of the house, hand-cup wavering above her head, still dripping water.

'Dragons, young 'uns,' she yelled. 'Orange and black all over my sheets. Horrible.'

She retched into the cauliflowers, the similar colours causing some trouble when cleaning up operations began. Mrs Neech put her arm round her, and said, 'There, there, dear, it's alright now,' and took her for a cup of tea. The newts, poor things, were disposed of, to our great annoyance.

'They got no right to treat them beautiful creatures like that,' moaned Johnny. He received his usual leather belt thrashing when his father came home, but was philosophical, despite the pain.

'Never mind,' he said. 'Plenty more where they came from.'

The newts he meant, but it was the same for thrashings.

His next hiding was not long after. The Council had planted young trees, about seven feet tall and supported by posts, in the verges of our road. Johnny was whirling a rope round his head in an attempt to lassoo Arthur, an idea he had gotten from cowboy films at the Regal, but he let go of the noose too soon. Inevitably it caught in one of the saplings and

Johnny pulled hard to yank it free. Inevitably the tree snapped and fell. As he bent to recover his rope he was surprised to feel a buffet on his head, so strong that he fell down and bawled with pain. The Council foreman, passing on his bicycle, had seen all, and administered swift punishment if not justice.

'I'll tell my father,' yelled Johnny through his tears.

'He didn't mean to do it,' Billy ventured, keeping well out of reach.

'That don't make no difference,' snarled the foreman. 'What's done's done. And you shut up unless you want your ear clipped as well.'

He cycled to Johnny's house and we all knew what would follow. His father erupted through the front door with red face and loud voice, belt swinging, and dragged him inside, leathering him as he went. At each blow his son screamed that he had not meant to damage the tree but it made no difference. Lack of intention meant nothing to Mr Strowger, never the philosopher.

'He really didn't mean no harm,' Billy shouted above the din. Mr Strowger paused, swinging his arm in his direction.

'You want some too? Clear off.'

It was two thrashings inside a week. Mr Strowger certainly did not spare the rod, or in his case, the leather belt.

Bicycle Advent

'Hey, what do you think you're a doing of? Blast me, you've stopped my water. Clear off afore I clout yer ear.'

The gang looked up to see a tall, well built middle aged woman running towards them, waving a copper stick in her large hands.

'Run,' said Billy. 'Cross to the other side. She won't want to get her feet wet.'

And so it proved. The angry housewife stopped on her bank and cursed, but the boys were safe.

'Must get her water from the stream,' said Roy. 'She's just had her supply restored. Dam's broken.'

It was Barsham Brook, Nelson's stream, that we had dammed, at the limit of our range. Until the coming of the bicycle, three miles there and three miles back was about as far as we could go when to walk was the only way to get anywhere. There were frequent trains and buses but there was no money for fares, and we wanted to go mainly into the meadows and woods that surrounded us, so public transport was of little help. We were slow walkers, averaging about two miles an hour. The countryside was so full of interest and much of the time was spent watching the birds and land creatures, and examining wild flowers. There were ditches to be jumped, ponds to be fallen into and trees to be climbed. Every expedition was full of interest and excitement and we were never bored.

Holly Bridge over the river Hundred was another common destination in the opposite direction, and just about the three miles. The water was usually swift and so no good for twig dropping races, for by the time you rushed to the other side of the bridge your stick was well downstream. Damming the river was the main excitement. Turves, clods of mud, stones and lumps of wood were gradually built into walls, starting from the edges and making them high and strong so as to resist the rush of water as the gap narrowed. Then, two sets of feet stood in the central space, and everybody else dropped their loads at the same time in front of their legs. It never worked, for the stream would be held up only for minutes before it outflanked our dam, poured round the sides and broke the centre. There was just too much water.

Things changed with the advent of the bicycles, most of them ASPs, All Spare Parts. They were cobbled together from bits and pieces gathered from the dump in Boney's Island, Muddy Hales' scrap yard and many less legal places. They were cheap but had disadvantages. Johnny, waiting in the Old Market, was injured in a very sensitive spot when his front wheel fell out and the forks dropped to the ground. I was lucky. Grandfather had just died and grandmother came to live with us, willing to spend the little bit of money he left her.

So I had a new, shiny black and chrome Dayton machine, the envy of the road. I suspected Dad's hand in the matter, first in twisting his mother in law's arm, and then in the actual purchase, for it was named after Daytona sands in Florida. There it was that Englishmen like Sir Malcolm Campbell and adopted Englishmen like Sir Henry Seagrave, both boyhood heroes, kept breaking the world land speed record.

I was not going to break any records. The cycle was heavy, a-sit-up-and-beg model, built to last, with rod brakes, no gears and a chain that could have served a steam engine. It was bought big, like shoes, in order that I would not grow out of it quickly. Dad fixed wooden blocks to the pedals so that I could reach them and often puffed himself out teaching me to ride. Then came visits to the rhododendrons at Blythburgh and the Black Swan at Homersfield, where I was not allowed in the building and had to sup my lemonade in the garden with him.

The coming of the bicycles increased our range. Instead of three miles, we could now go fifteen or even twenty miles from home, making round trips of up to forty miles possible. Lowestoft, Yarmouth and other large towns were not popular destinations - 'they'll pinch your bike'- was the common fear. Arthur had heard that a boy in Lowestoft got his wheels caught in the tram lines and had to cycle to the terminus to have his machine released. So we penetrated even greater ranges of countryside. There was an unexpected spin off since we found that we could escape much more quickly from pursuing adults who wished to punish us for alleged misdeeds. Provided the cycle had been left in a suitable position and we mounted quickly enough, nobody on foot stood a chance of catching us. Roy, copying cinema cowboy heroes, perfected a running mount. Just as they ran beside trotting horses and vaulted on, so did Roy scramble onto his machine and he taught us all this trick of swift departure.

But there were disadvantages. As pedestrians we were able to take time to observe and examine as we wandered about, unwittingly allowing the lasting influence of the beautiful countryside and skyscape in which we lived to take root in our souls. With little traffic it was still possible to look around as we cycled, but something had gone. Only the walker has the chance to see and appreciate all in his narrow but well observed world. The other loss was of much more immediate consequence. Bicycles needed to keep to roads and tracks and were useless on long grass or cultivated land, so there was a much greater chance of being caught by people in cars. No longer could we scamper off into the fields, sure that nobody would continue the chase.

And so we began to learn another lesson – that life is roundabouts and swings, and more pertinently, that some problems were solved, but others presented, by the advent of the bicycle.

Bits of Celluloid

Have you ever been asked by children you do not know to buy a cinema ticket for them with their own money? It was the only way Roy and I could get to see White Zombie in the Regent at Lowestoft just before the war. It was an 'A' classified film and as we were ten years old, we could enter only if accompanied by an adult.

So we stood outside with our sixpences (two and a half pence) and asked people going in if they would buy tickets for us. It was common practice and we soon found a willing couple. Once in the dark that had always been so friendly, we thanked them and separated, and although the attendants might notice us on our own they said nothing. Even the manager ignored us so long as we behaved well. He should have taken notice, for we were wholly scared.

White Zombie was full of bodies rising from the ground to terrorise the community and has haunted me all my life, enabling sharp recall of the disturbance of the granite chippings on the graves. First there were small cracks and pieces of stone tumbling away from a little hill. Then came a clutching hand with its crooked fingers grasping at the air, followed by a decaying head with staring eye sockets riveted on us. The rest of the body continued, chippings falling from it, clickety click.

We were hardened devotees of 'the pictures' and thought we had seen it all, but this terrified us into ducking behind the seat during the worst bits. Roy wanted to leave.

'Can't do that,' I said. 'We have to get our money's worth. It'll get better in a little while.'

But it got worse. The bodies began stumping about.

'Can't come off the screen and get you, can they?' asked Roy.

'They're only bits of celluloid,' I said with more conviction than I felt.

At the end we paused in the foyer, summoning our courage to get home.

'It's dark,' said Roy. 'We'd better run.'

Dashing out of the Regent at the top of Old Nelson Street, we ran down London Road North into Milton Road, past Swatman's sweet shop. The isolated gas lamps gave only feeble pools of light and there were few people about. We crossed the road to avoid those we did see in case they were zombies, just risen to get us. Then we remembered the hospital and stopped.

'Dead'uns,' I said. 'Yeah. There'll be dead'uns there. Go another way.'

'Thought they were only bits of celluloid,' said Roy.

'Best take no chances,' I answered. So we ran back to Arnold Street, walked quietly into Regent Road in case anybody came out of the cop shop, and raced to the Clapham Road crossroads. We kept together in the middle of the road as we passed Bobbins the butcher and Allerton's greengrocery. Zombies might be hiding in the doorways.

At home grandmother asked,

'What's the matter? Has somebody been chasing you?'

'No,' I gasped. 'Had a race with Roy.'

'Who won?'

'We both did.'

I dashed up the two pair of stairs to the attic, the tiny paraffin lamp with its white shade trembling in my hand, scrambled into my pyjamas and whizzed into bed, pulling the blankets over my head. The bits of celluloid followed and held a coven beneath me, deciding the best way to suck my blood. It was a long time before they moved away.

Nine Years Old

Smoking was very attractive. All the grown ups seemed to do it. Cinema screens and printed papers were filled with examples of elegant men and women who smoked, ladies often using a long holder.

'Their doctors told them to keep away from cigarettes,' said Billy. Arthur pointed out that there were three separate albums of film stars issued in the thirties with Player's cigarettes, and that only Marlene Dietrich was portrayed smoking.

We were satisfied with that for the moment and continued with our passion for collecting a full set of fifty of the current cards. There was one inside every packet of Medium Navy Cut cigarettes, and they were printed with an adhesive over the lettering on the back so that they could be stuck into the albums, which cost a penny (1/2p).

The details on the rear were repeated under the space where the card was irretrievably fixed. This has repercussions today. A set that is loose, not having been stuck down, is worth much more than the series in the albums. Nobody has yet devised a satisfactory method of removing the cards without damage.

Collecting cigarette cards was not a seasonal pastime like conkers, marbles or tops. It lasted through the years and was given up only as adolescence approached, and sometimes not even then. There was great competition to be the first to complete a set, and vigorous swap sessions were common. If others knew you needed just the last one or two to finish, then the price would rise from the usual one for one to one for five or more. You did not mind if it concluded your set. John Player made sure that the majority of collectors had their fifty before the series was changed.

Also issued in the thirties were Film Stars, first and second series (1934), The Kings and Queens of England, Civil Aeroplanes (both 1935), Motor Cars (1936), Cricketers (1938). As the war approached, there came exciting albums of Modern Naval Craft (1939) and Aircraft of the Royal Air Force (1938), including the Hurricane and Spitfire that were to win the Battle of Britain. The details given of these new fighters were surprisingly full but the maximum speed of the Spitfire was not released.

When a new issue appeared, cards left over from the old one were used in games. One card was balanced at an angle against a wall and others flicked to knock it down. The boy who did so took all the cards on the ground. Or a card would be placed flat and the winner was he who threw his card underneath.

Eventually, as the manufacturers knew well, boys, and sometimes girls, would want to smoke, but the prohibition by adults was fierce and punishment horrendous. So when we started, great care was taken not to arouse suspicion. We met in a six sided concrete pill box about half a mile along the Ellough Road, a defence against invasion in the first world war. It was barely visible from the highway since it stood in a pit, and brambles and old man's beard had grown tall around the entrance. We had no money

for cigarettes, and if we had tried to buy some the shopkeeper would have reported us to the police and probably to our parents as well. So we collected thrown away dog ends that contained real tobacco, the filter tip not being in great use then. We also had some dried and crushed raspberry leaves, and some similarly treated yellow coltsfoot from the railway embankment. Paper in which to roll the tobacco was a problem. India paper from a quality Bible was supposed to be good, but none of us dared risk the wrath, human and divine, that might fall on us if we desecrated the Holy Book. So we were reduced to the hard sulphite toilet paper that was sold then. Even that was difficult since in our homes newspaper cut into a convenient size was in use, holed at the corner and strung on a nail. Eventually we persuaded one of our richer friends into giving us a few sheets without divulging our purpose. The mixtures were rolled in several rounds of paper for we had no glue. Then the smoking began.

It is hard to say what we expected. For grown ups smoking seemed very pleasurable but it most certainly was not for us. Within minutes the pill box filled with fumes and we began to cough and splutter. Arthur rushed outside to be sick over the cow parsley that the girls called Queen Anne's lace, and Roy and Billy turned green and had the most awful feeling of nausea.

'I think I'm going back to the cards and leave the fags alone,' said Arthur between retches. 'The only good thing about cigarettes is the cards.'

I agreed. I have never smoked since, but it still pleases me to say when asked, 'No. Gave up when I was nine years old.'

Big Brian

'Stop that! What d' yer think you're doing?'

Big Brian was in charge of the swimming pool and he had a right to be angry.

We had watched as a platoon of uniformed soldiers marched down to the pool and paid for entrance and use of the big room changing facilities. They marched to the shallow end dressed only in what appeared to be black shorts, carrying towels, flannels and soap.

'What's the flannel and soap for?' asked Roy. We soon found out. Their sergeant bawled orders and the soldiers sat down with their feet in the water, rubbed soap on the flannels and began to wash. As they rinsed away the suds Big Brian appeared. The sergeant, still in his uniform, did not acknowledge him and his men continued to wash. Brian rushed up to him,

'You stop that at once, d' yer hear?'

The sergeant still took no notice until Brian grabbed him in a headlock.

'You got five seconds to stop those men from using my pool as a municipal wash house or in you go.'

It was plain that the men were enjoying the scene and none of them made any effort to help, so their commander, submitting to Big Brian's much superior height and weight, told them to stop. When released by the fuming pool supervisor, he smoothed his trousers and battle top and ordered his platoon out.

'You will be hearing from the colonel about this,' was his parting shot.

Big Brian's reply was, and is, unprintable. He was proud of 'The Bathing Place' which had brick built male and female communal changing rooms at one penny (1/2p), private cubicles at tuppence (1p) and not available to children, free lavatories and a small office. The concrete surround had two sets of wooden steps faced with rope matting, one at each end. Diving boards completed the equipment, both at the deep end, one just above the water and the other six feet high. Their use was restricted at low tide, for the pool was a part of the river, from which it was separated by a stout wooden fence. Most people, not liking the greasy feel of the gravel bottom at low tide, tried to swim at high tide, when there would be about three and a half feet of water, deepening to seven feet at the other end. Printed tide tables were available and the temperature in degrees Fahrenheit was chalked up daily. The premises were spotless, for Brian was a stickler for cleanliness and rules, and among these was the prohibition of trips into the river.

It was impossible to climb over the six feet of boarding from the water, and beneath was a skirt of small mesh wire netting that was anchored in the river bed. What Brian never seemed to realise was that the netting had been cut and rolled back, so that all the swimmer had to do was duck under the fence and he was in the river. But Brian kept a sharp watch, so

what we did was to have a lookout who would tell us when to move. On returning you had to fend for yourself, helped by a hollowed out knot, which gave a limited view of the passage from which Brian might issue at any time. The rule was designed to improve safety, for swimmers suddenly appearing in front of a boat were in danger. It was exciting to go into the river, for the water was clear to the bottom, and the plants growing there would trail with the tide.

Big Brian earned extra money by teaching youngsters to swim. He was a very successful teacher and his lessons were a great spectacle.

'He's got a new kid,' said Billy. 'Poor little devil. Yeah. I'm glad my parents don't have enough money for it.'

After preliminary land based instruction in the breaststroke Brian took his pupil to the deep end, where he hung a small padded horse collar round her neck. It was roped to a stout pole that he held in the air. The child climbed down the steps at the deep end.

'Now,' roared Brian, 'start the breast stroke.'

He ran along beside the water, lowering and raising the collar, so that his pupil kept disappearing below the surface, coming up for air and a splutter every few seconds. Such were the times that no protest was allowed, and nearly all of Brian's clients learned to swim very quickly. It was that or drowning by dipping, like the witches of old.

Perhaps it was the fear that my own parents might scrape the money to subject me to this ordeal that made me anxious to learn without Brian's help. It was tea time, about five o'clock, and everybody had gone home. I was in the pool by myself on a rising tide. Attempting to get out, I walked towards the steps at the shallow end and found that the water was too deep for me to reach them. So many people kept to the sides of the pool that the gravel had worn into a depression six inches deep. In the middle I was safe, with the water up to my neck, but could not get out. I was not worried, for I knew that the tide was on the turn and within half an hour would allow me to escape, or Brian would return and rescue me. But I did not want to wait and summoned up enough courage to try the breaststroke to the steps a few feet away. I was surprised to reach them so easily that I considered the matter and then turned and swam back to the middle. I had learned to swim without Big Brian's help.

Thinking Bats

'But why do they always fly over the top?' Arthur moaned. 'No matter how late or how high we raise the net we never catch any.'

It was true. The little gang had always been fascinated with bats, ever since they found half a dozen when they raised the font cover at Weston Church, though they lacked the courage to handle them. Certainly these were not the bloodsuckers of Dracula mythology, but it was as well to be careful.

'You never know,' added Arthur.

But now it was different. Mother had beaten fishing nets at Lowestoft in her single days, the repaired articles helping the fleet to continue its fabulous catches of silver darlings. When she married, she brought lengths of the tan one inch mesh net with her and used it to keep the blackbirds off the strawberries. Without her knowledge the boys had cut a piece about ten feet long and six feet wide. It had been attached to two long poles with nails and string, and taken to the corner of the block of four houses round which the bats circled endlessly at dusk. They waited, with all the anticipation of the hunter for his prey, although they had no intention of any harm.

'Now,' said Billy as a bat neared them. Roy and Arthur pushed the net into the air and the creature rose effortlessly above it.

'You said too soon,' complained Roy. 'Let us decide when to raise the net.'

The outcome was even worse. The two boys pushed up the net at different times with the result that only a squashed polygon was there for bats to negotiate.

'Let me have a go. We ought to be able to get some. They'll never be able to see the net in this light,' said Billy.

'I heard they were blind, anyway, so what difference does the dusk make?' added Arthur. Billy agreed with him that he would give the signal. The bat drew swiftly closer and when it was not more than a couple of feet away he shouted and the net flew up. Again the creature whizzed over the top and they put down the net to think. It made little difference what they did. No matter how close the bats were before the net rose, they sailed under or over so easily. One of them had executed a lightning turn of ninety degrees to evade capture.

'I can't make it out,' said Billy. 'I'll ask my Dad.'

But he was unable to solve the mystery. He watched them raise the net several times and commented, 'It's clear that they know the net is there and they have the agility to avoid it. But how they know is another matter.'

And so the investigation rested until after the war. Research then showed that bats had a very effective form of sonar, emitting high pitched sounds that reflected back to them and enabled them to avoid obstacles.

The boys' other attempts to capture flying creatures were more successful. They borrowed an old meat safe. This was a cylinder made of bent plywood, about six inches long and twelve inches in diameter, with zinc gauze at the top. It was placed over meat to keep off flies. The plan was to tip it slightly to one side and support it with a stick so that a bird could hop in easily to eat the food placed as bait. A trail of food was laid outside the safe, a trail leading into danger. When the quarry was well underneath, the string attached to the stick was pulled, the safe fell and the bird was captured. That was the theory. They hid behind the privet hedge and waited.

'There's a robin,' whispered Roy. Partly tame from its contact with human beings the unsuspecting redbreast landed near the breadcrumbs. When it reached the safe it paused.

'It's not going in,' said Arthur. 'It knows.'

But at that moment Roy pulled the string and the bird was inside, fluttering in terror.

'What shall we do with it?' asked Arthur.

'Let it go.'

This they did. They had found a successful way of catching birds, but the ease of the operation soon made it boring.

'At least the bats had us thinking,' said Billy. Roy laughed, 'Think better than we do,' he said.

This Big Pig

Roy stood with his back to the sty where the sow was penned, while at the other end of the row the auctioneer was rapidly pushing up prices. The boy's nimble fingers silently worked the catch till it grated open, attracting one of the drovers, stationed there especially against marauders.

'What you doin, there, boy? Clear off afore you feel the weight o' my stick.'

Roy dodged, skilfully avoiding the bulky stockman, already slowed by too much beer and too many pickles in the Railway Arms. As he fled he bumped into Arthur.

'Hey, look where you're going, you,' he yelled, hitting out. In a moment the two were rolling on the floor shouting and grunting, and the drover ran over to separate them. He raised his stick but the pair broke away. During the 'fight' Billy took advantage of the commotion to swing open the gate of the sty, walloped the sow and fled. In a moment all was confusion.

Boys, drovers and farmers streamed towards the gate, following the sow which had headed unerringly for freedom, aided by the sticks of urchins who appeared as if by magic at every junction, guiding her towards Station Road. Not many people were about but those that were quickly turned into the grounds of the Baptist or Methodist churches as the cry, 'Pig out,' was raised.

She had a good start and was up to the top of the road well ahead of the boys, bicycles, and following van. At the crossroads a woman screamed, picked up her baby from its pram and dashed into Spashett's, slamming the door. There was no need to worry. The sow continued in a straight line, as if drawn by the magnet of the market stalls. Perhaps she scented the vegetables, for it was at this point that she slowed down. A spilled potato attracted her and under the stall she ferreted. The proprietor, made of sterner stuff than many of the townsfolk, lashed at her with his boot and she responded with a toss of the head that took away one of the trestles.

Cabbages and onions, carrots and potatoes rolled into the road as she made off again, running well. A baby Austin braked hard, tyres squealing in an attempt to avoid the bouncing vegetable cornucopia, and the pig van, speeding to collect the sow, crashed gently into its rear, glass tinkling from front and back lights. The Austin driver swore at the stallholder, who swore at the van driver. Then they all swore at one another and cursed the pig that had sensibly withdrawn from the melee.

The manager of Dewhurst's was in his cold room when he heard a yell and glanced back to see a woman climbing onto his counter.

'Come off it, lady,' he called, and was ready to strengthen his language when the sow snuffled round the end of the chopping bench. He gasped in alarm, being used to pork, not live meat, and turned for the door but it was too late. The sow, frightened by the woman's screams and the bloodstained cleaver she threw at it, dashed round the bench again before it found the exit, banging the cold room door shut as it did so. The catch dropped on the outside.

'Let me out,' roared Jones. His boss had often reproved him for failing to secure the catch when he went in.

'You will freeze to death with your own meat one day,' he told him. Now it had happened. He wondered if the silly woman would remember where he was, and turned up the temperature control behind the carcasses of pigs.

'Be those boys again,' he mumbled to himself. 'Another sow let loose'.

Nellie wandered on, slowly when unmolested, swiftly when aroused. Outside Keeble the chemist she sniffed at an infant left in a pram. Next day the rumour was that she had eaten a baby and people as far away as Halesworth reportedly refused to eat sausages. They would have had better cause had they seen the butcher's actions a few days before. He had been distracted while making sausages and the electric machine had nicked his thumb. An astonished Billy watched while he laughed, holding it over the churning mixture and letting the blood drip in.

'That'll give it a bit of flavour, eh, boy?'

The smell from the chemist's did not please Nellie and she doubled across to the weighbridge between the Town Hall and the White Swan. Her weight set the bridge swinging and this, coupled with its deep patterned iron surface had her down for the first time. But not for long. As the mob approached she was away again, past the Church tower and down the lane which led through the Co-op premises. In the narrow space she managed to upset a boy pulling a trolley. Boxes, wrappings and shoes fell about in leathery confusion and impeded pursuit once more.

'She's making for the sale ground,' shouted one of the farmers. 'Take the van down the end of Printer's lane and you'll catch her.'

The vehicle roared off down Station Road and soon pulled up, blocking the space. Too late Nellie saw the danger and swung round. It was no good. A massed barricade of bicycles and sticks was moving steadily nearer and after a few tentative sorties she made her way into the van. Soon, with much protesting, she was back in her pen and the auctioneer appeared.

'Excellent sow, fine runner,' he announced and she was quickly sold, the last lot of the day. While the men were busy Billy leaned over the sty and scratched her back.

'You're a good 'un, Nellie,' he whispered. 'Best run we've had for a long time.'

From her grunts and squeaks he felt she understood. The outing had clearly been enjoyed by this Big Pig.

Den for Burning

'Does your father keep a shop?'

Miss Burton, our excellent, well respected teacher of English, affectionately known as 'Granny', kept me after class.

'No, Miss Burton, he works at the Shell Mex depot.'

'I wondered, because on Saturday I saw you hauling a trolley loaded with cardboard boxes through the town.'

'That's right, Miss Burton. The boxes were for our bonfire on 5 November.'

You must not call her 'Miss'. It was always to be her full name.

'It takes away your individuality,' she said. It was just another of her teaching points which stuck and is always put into practice. She smiled.

'You are early. It's only mid October.'

She was right. We started collecting from shops before the town gangs began to do the same. Some traders could be persuaded to keep their inflammable waste for us if they were sure we would come regularly on specified days. Besides, it was a long haul to our road on the outskirts of the town, and it took us twice the time to collect loads, although we persuaded ourselves that our early start was because we were better organised. Boys pulling four wheelers loaded with rubbish were a familiar sight in the weeks before the great night. It was looked on as the glorious fifth between the end of the summer holidays and Christmas.

'Four wheelers' were go-carts made of two pairs of old pram wheels from the dump and some wood. It was not unusual for boys to watch out for families where baby carriages - the posh name - might soon be discarded. Parents or other adults needed persuasion to bore a hole in the centre of the front axle to make steering possible, and a wooden box from a greengrocer was added as a secure seat. Loops of cord on each end of the front axle meant that the cart could be accurately manoeuvred, especially if helped by placing your feet on either side of the axle, near the wheels.

When the boxes were safely home in our back garden we stood them on old bits of lino (linoleum, a cheap floor covering) to stop the damp getting in. Then, when the grown ups were out, we made them into a den. Dens were very popular and we had several dotted about the countryside, but this one was in our back garden. It was special.

'You keep watch, Arthur,' said Billy. 'If anybody come, start whistling.

'Why should I always do it? I want to help with the den.'

'Because you're more afraid than we are so you notice danger quicker. We'll swap in a minute.'

And so, with great pains to keep the real operation secret, the boxes were arranged in a rectangle with a central area open. Old planks were put over the top of this space and cardboard placed on them, followed by full boxes. Roy was once inside, helping to support the roof when it all fell in and he was quite ickeny about it. But we were now experienced and there were no accidents. It took about an hour to finish and from the outside it seemed like a neatly arranged pile of boxes, covered with a tarpaulin borrowed with permission from Dad's work place. That was what everybody was supposed to think, but for us it was the most secret and wonderful den we ever had.

Entrance was at the back, concealed from the house. In the other direction was the thick shelter of a tall privet hedge. The tarpaulin needed lifting slightly to reveal what looked like just another cardboard box of rubbish. But it was empty and two sides were now hinged to provide access to crawlers. We all scrambled in.

'It's dark,' complained Arthur.

'I suppose you were expecting electric light,' said Roy.

'And here it is,' announced Billy as he turned a switch. Arthur goggled. 'That's a six volt battery. Where did you get it?'

'From the wireless shop. My Dad got it for us.'

'Then he'll know about the den.'

'Course he will. He got the tarpaulin, too. Don't worry. He won't tell.'

And he did not. Neither about the one in his garden, nor about the others he suspected in the countryside. And this one would soon be the den for burning.

Treacle Tin Banger

It was always a problem to find money for Guy Fawkes celebrations. The Standard Fireworks poster in baker Farman's window near the railway crossing deceived us only once. From a distance it announced, 'A BOY WANTED HERE', and we thought the answer had come. One of us would get the job and we would be rich, but on closer inspection other words became visible so that the poster read, 'A BOY WANTED some Standard Fireworks. He got them HERE.' It was early training in the importance of reading the small print.

The cheapest and most violent banger, the Little Demon, was only a halfpenny (1/5p) but that meant, even with pooled pocket money and the little bits we managed to earn we could buy only a few fireworks. Then came the discovery of the treacle tin banger and the result was something like Newton's apple falling on our economically desperate heads.

We had to obtain a treacle tin, or more correctly, a tin that had contained two pounds weight of Lyle's Golden Syrup. The containers were identical with those on sale today except for the bar code and 907g metric marking. There was the same intricate green and gold decoration and the oval name plate enclosing the picture of the dead lion and the bees, with its quotation from the book of Judges: 'Out of the strong came forth sweetness.' We knew the answer better than the Philistines who could get it only from Samson's girl friend.

The tin we found had already been rinsed out to get at the last traces of syrup but we cleaned it again to make sure it would work properly. A small hole was then bored with a bradawl in the circular side of the tin about a quarter inch from the base. Two knobs of calcium carbide were put inside. A tablespoon of water followed, but we found urine would do and was less trouble than going indoors for the tap. The lid was then firmly clamped down and after a five second wait a light was applied to the hole, whereupon the lid blew off with a most satisfying explosion, sometimes reaching a height of forty feet.

The calcium carbide and water produced acetylene gas that was highly explosive when mixed with air. The beauty of it was that the chemical was usually free, since many people, including Dad, used it in cycle lamps. It was also used for sailing lights on the fishing boats at Yarmouth and Lowestoft, where, we suspected, Dad obtained his supply. We calculated that even if we had to buy the carbide, we got 20 bangs for a penny instead of two with fireworks.

At first the dogs barked and people complained but Dad told them it was practice for the coming war.

'Hitler's bombs'll sound louder than that,' he said. They soon got used to it but after a few days the whole thing palled. The ease with which the explosions were produced, and their failure to arouse even canine protest due to constant repetition, took the edge off the pleasure. There were, however, certain developments. Several tins were used at once, producing half a dozen linked explosions a bit like anti-aircraft gunfire, and rousing the dogs and populace again. Dad, who believed the warnings of Winston Churchill, continued his support.

'The boys will have to get used to explosions,' he said. 'So will we all. Let them enjoy themselves while they can.'

A further development led us into a great error. Flushed with the success and delight of the operation, we arrived early before school one morning and settled ourselves inside the high laurel hedge. There we wedged and tied one tin on its side in a V shaped branch and prepared to fire, reckoning that we had enough carbide and water to fire at least twenty lids. The first girl pedalled slowly up the slope only to be shaken out of her sweaty morning reverie by an enormous bang and the clatter of a metal disc against the spokes of her front wheel. White and trembling she wobbled on her way, sensibly not caring to investigate lest worse befall. Cycle wheels, but no people, were struck with regular accuracy and success went to our heads.

'Here comes Holly,' said Harry. 'Give him the last one. He'll never catch us.'

The tin was primed and the lid pressed firmly down. Holly, one of the most prickly of masters, rode unsuspectingly nearer, panting a little.

'Now,' whispered Harry. With a cannon like boom the lid flew out of the hedge and into the front wheel of the astonished master. As we scampered out of the laurel he roared his anger and we could imagine him tearing into the leaves to find nothing there.

But he was cleverer than we thought and we learned another lesson, to stand some of us in good stead. Never under estimate your enemies. Guessing our plan, he rode quickly to the boys' entrance and waited for us. We almost knocked him down as we rounded the corner, our arms full of incriminating evidence. He was always imaginative and very practical over punishment and made us roll the cricket square with the horse roller for an hour after school. It was heavy work but became enjoyable as it went on. Dad said that if we fired near people he would give us no more carbide.

'You'll have to fire at human beings soon enough,' he said sadly. 'And with something more deadly than treacle tin bangers.'

New Blood

The gang tramped its heavy booted, mud clinging way over the haunted heath, through the Bible-black night, in disorderly and disconsolate fashion. It was the evening after Guy Fawkes, always a depressing low after the heady elation of bonfire and fireworks, especially since a Little Demon had gone off in Eric's hand and sent him to the doctor. Fortunately he was only bruised, although he had cried all evening.

Poking about among the empties revealed a half burned sparkler that eventually sputtered to a damp and dismal daylight conclusion after half a box of matches had been wasted on it.

'Good job they're not our matches,' said Arthur.

A cone shaped Vesuvius, however, with the blue touch paper missing, spat lava immediately a light was applied and almost burned the thick skinned hand of Shash, who fell over with the shock while Roy kicked the spurting monster away.

Apart from that, the day had been worse than a wet Saturday and soon after dark they began to play 'Jack, Jack, show your light.' Shash ran off into the dark as fast as he could to make the most of his one minute start. The rest of the gang counted to a quick sixty followed with frequent shouts of 'Jack, Jack, show your light'. He was then bound by the rules to give one flash on his torch. But even the excitement of pursuit in the pitch black East Anglian countryside palled in the post fifth of November depression. So they trod warily over the heath, keeping close together lest it live up to its reputation. They did not need ghostly stimulation.

Shash cursed as he tripped over. 'Whittaker's laying man traps now,' he grumbled as he picked himself up. 'That's illegal, that is.'

A moment later violent blue flashes lit the sky ahead, confirming all the rumours and their own worst fears about the haunted heath. As one the gang turned and ran, slowing only at the hedge.

'I always said we shouldn't come across the heath after dark,' yelled Shash. 'You never take no notice o' me. That's the ghost of the heath and that's after us.'

As they tore through the bushes Billy tried to restore a little sense.

'There's no ghost. We're all daft. There's some electric cables go across there, near the headland, just where we were. There must be something wrong with them, or something must have hit them.'

'Perhaps that was a bat,' suggested Arthur.

'Now you are talking daft,' said Roy. 'Everybody know bats don't hit nothing, not even in the dark. Don't you remember how we tried to catch them with fishing net on sticks?'

With great caution the boys crept slowly over the heath once more. They kept together, close by the ditch and hedge, fearful despite Billy's scientific explanation. Maybe something more than electricity was involved. You never knew.

'It was about here,' said Shash, worried now that Black Shuck, the devil dog of East Anglia, might be around. 'A bit o' wire wrapped itself round my feet and I threw it in the air. Here's another bit.'

He held up a ring of thin wire about two feet in diameter.

'That's from the tyres we burned last night,' said Roy.

Whittaker, relenting perhaps because of the good the bonfire ash would do his field, allowed them to have the fire near the headland provided they cleared up. Taylor gave them a load of old cycle tyres and they put the left over wires in the ditch.

'Let's see if we can do it again,' said Billy, throwing a wire ring forward into the air. Nothing happened.

'You're not strong enough,' sneered Shash. 'Let me try.'

Suddenly blue and white flashes appeared, momentarily lighting the boys' faces and the electricity cables ahead. Within seconds they pulled wires out of the ditch by the score and the soft East Anglian darkness began to spurt and flame in startling fashion as the power lines were hit again and again.

'All throw at once,' shouted Billy. 'One, two, three and go.'

The gang had never known such excitement and exhilaration. As usual, they became absorbed in the activity, and did not notice the doors opening on the Council estate until the householders moved nearer.

'That's that gang again, messing about with the lights and causing everyone trouble,' bawled Mr Strowger. 'They'll feel the weight of my belt in a minute.'

'Pack it in,' said Billy. 'Someone's coming.'

They stopped and heard Mr Strowger shout again.

'Terrible interference on my wireless.'

'Don't be daft, you old fool,' yelled Roy. 'That can't do nothing to a crystal set.'

'Stop cheeking him,' said Billy. 'You know it'll only make him worse. Come on. Run.'

Once again the gang rushed down the haunted heath, even little Arny finding it easy to outrun the half hearted posse who soon returned, grumbling, to the warmth of the fireside and Arthur Askey's Bandwagon programme.

Next day, in the after school dusk, Billy and Roy revisited the scene of the night flashes to find Shash chasing small boys away from the electricity cables.

'They were throwing wires at the lines,' he panted. 'Look what they've done. Everybody'll think it was us.'

Roy and Billy gazed in admiration. The younger boys had succeeded in balancing a bow shaped wire on the top cable. As the wind caught it, the wire dipped to one side and touched one of the lower cables. Each time there was a slight spark and crackle, and one of the street lights illuminated for a moment. Gently the wire alternated to and fro, the light coming on every four or five seconds.

'That's very good,' murmured Billy. 'Now that really is an achievement.'

He shouted to the youngsters, standing in a fearful group far enough away to escape into their houses if need be.

'Don't be afraid. Come and join us. We need some new blood.'

So Far in Blood

'I heard my father say there was an old air gun in the shod,' said Johnny. Better than these catapults.'

He took from his pocket a Y shaped bit of hazel, the preferred wood, although any other tree could have supplied equally useful forked branches. A quarter inch square piece of black elastic about five inches long was bound with kite string to each end of the split forks, and in the middle it was threaded through a square of leather. A rounded pebble such as David took from the brook fitted into this small pouch and was pulled back as far as it would go without breaking the expensive elastic. Johnny was a particularly good shot though we all doubted his ability to fell someone like Goliath. He needed a new challenge, which explained his interest in the air gun.

'Let's find it. Get a rabbit or two. That should please them. Maybe they'll stop hitting me.'

But when the gun appeared from the muddle at the back of the shed it was plain that its best days were over. Even cleaned up and polished it looked a poor thing.

' You won't get many rabbits with that,' said Billy. 'Not unless I hold them down while you bang them on the head with it.'

Trials proved Billy correct. The pellets scrounged from home had a job to reach the house wall from the bottom of the garden.

It was then that fate took a hand. A black cat appeared, sauntering down the neighbour's garden path, ignoring everything. Now for us black cats were witches cats, despite the tiny bits of white bred into them to avoid the stigma. To hurt one was supposed to bring bad luck, but Johnny swung the gun towards the moving target and fired. The smack of the pellet on the unfortunate creature's body was distinct but we both knew no blood would be drawn. The poor animal jumped a couple of feet in the air, screeched violently and sped off like a rocket while we collapsed with laughter. Billy managed to hit a low flying sea gull but it swerved and flew on. We muttered about 'sportsmen' who needed the wide spread of a shotgun to hit anything.

As in all we did, a course of evil, once started, seemed to acquire a life of its own and we began to look for more interesting targets. Years later, when Shakespeare began his civilising influence on them, Billy came across one of the speeches of Richard III before Henry VII overwhelmed him at the battle of Bosworth Field in 1485. 'But I am in,' he said, 'so far in blood that sin will pluck on sin. Tear falling pity dwells not in this eye.'

So they hid behind the front privet hedge and looked for prey. Along came Fat Albert who worked for Major Took, the First World War hero who lived at the bottom of the hill. He was pushing a loaded wheelbarrow

and as he leaned into the job his trousers shone tightly on his bottom. Billy nodded and Johnny let fly, both boys relishing the smack of the pellet on the greasy corduroy.

'He'll never guess,' hissed Johnny. 'He don't know muck from rhubarb.'

But he did. He dropped the handles abruptly, drew in his breath, rubbed his bottom and looked round. The boys froze, but from the trajectory he guessed and ran towards them. Taking off fast they made for the back hedge, but their start was not enough and the two of them would be no match for Albert. His blood was up and he would massacre them. The alternative was to separate so he would get only one, but the code of loyalty prohibited that.

'Drop the gun,' said Billy.

'Why?' asked Johnny.

'Just do it, idiot.'

As expected, Fat Bertie picked it up and smashed it against the house wall before he turned towards them once more, but they were now over the difficult back hedge and might escape completely if he started to climb. He hesitated and Billy said,

'How do you know we didn't get you here so somebody could pinch your barrow? Major Took wouldn't be very pleased if he heard you'd been playing games with air guns and lost a valuable barrow as a result. Might cost you a month's wages or even the sack. And we've just found two big sticks.'

'Where?' said Johnny, but if Fat Bertie heard him it made no difference. He ran to make sure his barrow was safe. It was, and so were we. We were not so far in blood after all.

Learning Better

The grown ups would have thought what we did to ants was a terrible thing, almost as bad as sadistic boys who sometimes pulled the legs off live flies or even frogs. One boy put a milk straw into the anus of a frog and blew it up like a balloon. It seemed a dreadful thing to do but the swollen creature soon returned to its normal size and hopped about its normal business. When we discovered the power of an old torch lens to concentrate the sun's rays, the ability to set paper and wood on fire soon palled, and the ants suffered. We followed them with the lens and literally burned them up. Their fate was quick. It was all over in a second, unlike the poisons that the adults occasionally put down, causing lingering death to many. It was just as well, however, that they never found out, any more than they did about the wasp races.

A stunned wapse was required, and since you wanted it to revive quickly, care was necessary. A loosely folded newspaper was ideal if used with not too much force. Then the wapse was picked up with tweezers, care being essential again because some of them feigned death, and had been known to take a well deserved revenge. If stung, we all knew that a wasp sting needed vinegar while a bee sting required the blue bag, used to bring whiteness to the washing. The only way to remember it was to say, Winegar for a Wasp and therefore the blue bag was for the bee.

If the poor creature was still stunned it was placed on a thin pointed flat stick about three inches long and half an inch wide, previously anointed with cycle puncture glue. This was a tricky operation. Speed was essential since the glue would dry rapidly and you wanted none of it on the wings. Worse, the wapses might revive before time and come whirring at you like avenging aliens in their yellow and black plated armour, knowing well who was responsible for their torment.

Then came the wait. Sometimes nothing happened, for the lucky wapses had been hit too hard and were dead, but we discovered that they were remarkably resilient and nearly always recovered fast and tried to fly. The stick boat would then zoom over the surface in the rain water butt. It was even possible to make the tiny craft go in a straight line if the wapse had been correctly positioned and a lightweight rudder fixed. Races were tried, but the wapses were so energetic that they reached the other side of the water butt almost as soon as the boats were released. Ponds offered larger areas on still days, but the creatures lost themselves in reed mace and bulrushes and died lingering deaths that we never intended. We were amazed at the power of the small insects and wondered about attaching hundreds of them on a board in front of a canoe.

It did not seem to us that we were doing anything cruel. Adults encouraged us to make wapse traps from two pound jam jars. A cut up apple core was put in the bottom of the jar, though anything fruity would do, followed by a couple of inches of water. A funnel made from paper was then fixed with a rubber band round the top of the jar. As the mixture fermented in hot sun, wapses would be attracted, crawling down the paper into the small air space between funnel and liquid. Inevitably they fell into the fruity soup below and drowned after hours of struggle. What we were doing was less cruel, for our wapses were killed quickly when we had finished with them. We scraped them off the boat, stood on the remains, and started again another day. Have you ever watched the slow death struggles of a wasp sprayed with a modern killer?

We also joined in the harsh treatment of animals in the stock markets, beating errant pigs and cattle with enthusiasm under the direction of our elders. Nobody had heard of animal rights or put forward any sort of environmental argument. We were products of our time, thoughtless country boys who grew up to learn better.

What Car?

'Car coming,' announced Roy as if it was an event. It was. Except on market days and a few hours on Saturdays it was something special for the road on the edge of the town. The car was special too.

'What is it?' continued Roy. 'Come on. I thought you knew all the cars in the album.'

The vehicle cruised slowly along, the driver occasionally putting his head out of the window.

'It's the doctor. He's looking for the Brindlewoods' house where Bernie died of the diphtheria last week. I'm glad I don't have to go in there. I walk on the other side of the road,' said Billy with a shudder. They both remembered how Mabel Kindred had died last year of the scarlet fever, and knew that more deaths from diphtheria were likely.

The car stopped and Doctor Evans disappeared into the house.

'Let's go and annoy Mrs Sheepshanks. We only need to sit outside.'

Roy sat on the four wheeler and Billy pushed until they reached the lady's house. She attended a service at the nearby village church nearly every day but it seemed to do her little good. Often she was to be seen at her front window, thinking she was hidden by the lace curtains, and nobody told her she was not. Her outline was clearly visible.

Now there was an unwritten rule when a ball was accidentally hit into a garden. The owner walked to the front door, apologised and politely asked if he could get it. The answer was usually, 'Yes, but please mind the flowers.'

Many of the householders told the children that they need not ask if they were careful to do no damage and the system worked well to everyone's advantage. But Mrs Sheepshanks was different. If the ball came over her hedge, she rushed out and confiscated it, so naturally the owner raced in to retrieve his property before she laid her hands upon it. He had no time for care with plants or flowers and nor did she, quite unnecessary mayhem being wrought twice. Recently she had been successful. Kenny, who wore shoes to school but who often went barefoot at other times, had kicked the ball into her garden and she had got there first. She bore her trophy into the house, proclaiming,

'I'll have all the balls that come in this garden,' but Kenny, with all the lewdness of ten years, shouted back, 'You won't get mine, Missus.'

Doctor Evans came out of the house, eyes to the ground.

'He's coming here. We're not doing anything wrong,' said Roy.

The car stopped and the much respected doctor, who had been Mayor of the town the year before, got out.

'And how would you two like to earn threepence (one and a half pence) each?'

'Yes please, Sir,' said Billy.

'Good. This road seems very untidy today and what I want you to do is to pick up all the litter and rubbish lying around and put it in a dustbin. Now, do you think you could do that for me please?'

'Yes Sir, we can,' answered Billy, eyeing the coins the doctor was counting out. 'We'll make a good job for you, Sir.'

He gave three pennies to Roy and three to Billy.

'Thank you, Sir,' said Billy. They began as soon as the doctor started the engine, and spurred on by his trust in them, soon cleared the road.

'Looks a lot better,' said Billy. 'And I've got threepence, two weeks' pocket money.'

'What was it then?' said Roy.

'What was what?'

'What car was it?'

'It was a Singer 11,' said Billy. Saloon. Same colour as the one in the cigarette card album. It's very modern with a four speed synchromesh gear box and a fluid flywheel that means the engine can be kept running in gear with the car standing still. Costs £245.'

'Doctors must be rich,' answered Roy. 'But I'm glad I know what car it is.'

A Good Start

'You missed,' screamed Arthur as Billy's hefty ash stick came down with a resounding thwack, missing the rat by an inch. It scrabbled and squirmed away, but Roy was ready and the unfortunate creature squealed in agony as his club broke its back. He hacked off the still quivering tail with his knife and added it to the pile. Barns and corn stacks were fruitful sources of the vermin and they could be killed at any time with the ready sanction of farmers. It was a change for the gang to have adult approval.

Rats' tails were one answer to absent or meagre pocket money, for they were worth a penny each at the dicky dealer's house next door to the Territorial Army Drill Hall. Arthur had an idea.

'Why don't we slip in a couple of the fine ends of parsnip roots. I heard tell that the girls who count them in some places don't like doing it and don't notice.'

'Maybe,' said Billy. ' But I can't see him falling for that.'

'Him' was a tall bearded man in greasy corduroys, abrupt and a bit frightening in his manner but he always paid up.

Rabbits were more seasonal and although they were trapped through the year with a running noose snare, Harvest provided a bonanza. The horse drawn sail binder clattered relentlessly nearer the middle of field. Each round decreased the area of standing corn where we knew the rabbits were hiding. We waited and watched. It seemed that our prey panicked on a given signal, for there would be up to forty rabbits bolting at the same time, in an excited yelling melee of old men, boys, dogs and a couple of guns. Amazingly, nobody was ever hurt.

Sixpence (two and a half p.) was the going price for a freshly killed rabbit from passers by, or hawked round the houses, but they usually finished in the pot at home, a nourishing and delicious two day meal a in hard time. We usually had the skin, worth a penny or tuppence (1p) at the dicky dealer's. Moleskins, or the undamaged bodies of recently killed animals, brought fourpence or even sixpence for a good specimen. The creatures refused to come out, however, and we killed only one in six years.

Spring brought primroses to sell to the shops, a penny a bunch, and violets, tuppence. Around Michaelmas there were blackberries, bullaces and crab apples at tuppence a pound, and 'dew fresh mushrooms' as the traders called them, might bring threepence. Shops were careful over mushrooms, needing to be sure that sellers knew the difference between delicacy and poison. We had to be careful, too, for Whittaker, the fungus cavalry, often patrolled his meadows in the early morning, or put a bull in with the cows to try and keep us out.

Shopkeepers sold at treble the price they paid but it was no good complaining or trying elsewhere, for there was a cartel with agreed rates. And boxed ears and clattered heads soon knocked business sense into clever dicks who tried to sell on the pavement outside the shop. We learned early the wiles of capitalism, and discovered that without a union there was always somebody who would accept a lower price. Those first in the market reaped the rewards, so it paid to be there before the competition, but no trader would agree to take our goods on a sole or regular basis.

Newspapers for the fish and chip shops made tuppence a stone, but after lugging fourteen pounds of News Chronicles into the town it was hardly worth it, even on a go cart. Proprietors would say they had enough, knowing that many boys would leave them rather than carry them back home.

The two stock markets that functioned each week provided an exciting source of income but competition was fierce. Some farmers would give sixpence or even a shilling (5p) for help with driving cattle or sheep a few miles to a nearby farm, since it was much cheaper than a lorry for short distances. If, however, you were suspected of freeing pigs from their pens to run riot in the town, the job would go to someone else. It was a hard choice.

The Common gate was another exciting and rewarding way of earning money. It was kept closed so that grazing horses would not stray and this meant that members of the Golf club had to stop their cars and open and shut the heavy gate, often in inches of horse trodden droppings and mud. Gangs added water from the ditches on dry days to make the passage worse. Small wonder then that most drivers were glad to have the gate opened and shut for them. At least threepence was the usual return, sixpence was not unusual, and shillings had been known. Sometimes we found abandoned golf balls on the Common and would offer these to people in the cars.

'We found a golf ball, Sir. Is it one of yours?'

Sometimes they gave a bit extra, sometimes not. If custom was slow, there was always the diversion of swinging on the gate. This pulled it down on its hinges, scraping the surface and increasing the chance of drivers asking us to open it.

The difficulty was that a gang was needed to fight off others who laid claim to the job. Our group would line up and start to throw stones as the enemy came within range, shouting, jumping up and down and screaming at the same time. When they wavered, we would charge and they would turn and run. The group in possession would usually win the fight without too much trouble. It was like a band of apes defending a food supply. A three hour stint on a Saturday or Sunday might mean the untold wealth of a shilling each, for nearly all golfers gave generously. Non payers might find the gate tied and wedged on their return, or have mud thrown at them. If a persistent car occupant showed signs of pursuit, everybody ran. We all knew that no adult could catch us if we had a good start.

Filthy Lucre

'What's the matter with him?' asked the holiday maker with the Kiss Me Quick cap. Billy's younger brother Colin was on all fours, peering into a surface water drain and crying his eyes out while Billy tried to lift it.

'Lost his penny down the drain, Sir. He was going to buy an ice cream.'

The man rummaged among his small change and gave Colin a penny.

'There you are, my boy. Dry your eyes. It's all better now.'

'Oh, Sir, that is very kind. Say thank you to the nice gentleman, Colin.'

The small boy mumbled thanks through his tears, looked up with the beginnings of a smile and set off for the ice cream parlour. The smallest cornet was a halfpenny, (1/5p) so Billy had one too. They came in pink or buff coloured biscuit cones with vanilla or strawberry ice cream so you had four choices, and the delicious concoction was plastered in and on by a smiling girl with a wooden spoon. Her ambition was clearly to see how much she could get on one cone. As soon as it was finished they returned to a different grating to try and get some money so Roy could have one too. The trick worked well, for most people on holiday were in generous mood, but problems arose when the same person saw the act for the second time. Running away was not an option since Colin was only four. Besides, flight was an admission of guilt, so they brazened it out between them.

'Honestly, Sir, he dropped the one you gave him on the way to the ice cream stall,' Billy would say, without much hope of belief, but nobody could prove anything so they got away with it. It would end that particular trick for the day. No matter, for most people stayed only a week in the seaside town, so a new audience was almost guaranteed every few days.

Roy's performance was more spectacular. He whitened his cheeks with French chalk from a cycle puncture kit and sat hunched forward on the sea wall. Then he spat blood on the concrete. It was so realistic that the first time she saw it, Gloria asked, 'Is something the matter? You haven't got the consumption, have you?'

'Course not,' said Billy with a laugh. 'He's having you on. It's those crimson cough drops again.'

Passers by were not so susceptible to this fraud, perhaps because they did not like the mess on the promenade and maybe they thought they might catch tuberculosis, a common and often fatal disease of the time.

Nevertheless it was worth a few coppers and the occasional sympathetic sixpence, and it was well nigh foolproof. Who was going to dabble in the gory gobs that Roy produced after a cough that seemed to begin in his lower intestine? When tackled about whether it was a right thing to do, Roy said it was no worse, and maybe better than the tricks played by the lady on the apple stall. She had beautiful red and green apples for sale, all with a splendid gloss in which you could almost see your face. That was at the point of display. If you lifted the canvas at the back, she could be seen spitting on the fruit and polishing away with her none too clean snot rag.

'Now she really could be spreading the consumption,' argued Roy.

There were more legitimate ways of earning seaside money during the summer holidays. It was still possible to take your go cart to the station of the London and North Eastern Railway and offer to help with luggage.

'Cart your bags for you, Sir,' was the cry. 'Sixpence. Much cheaper than a taxi and easier than lugging it around yourself.'

Care was needed or you finished up with a family who had ten cases and loved walking. They might direct you along the promenade to an address beyond the Claremont Pier and even into Kirkley or the outskirts of Pakefield, to say nothing of the Belle Vue park area in the other direction. Such customers would sometimes give you the address, set off along the prom, and you would find yourself on the doorstep waiting for what seemed like hours for your money. Others were sometimes very careful with their cash, like the man who took the wheels off the baby's pram before he put it on the train. To the collector who said, 'Where's the ticket for the pram?' he said, 'What pram? Prams have wheels.'

The beach was a good provider. If you were first in the morning, there was always money to be found under the Claremont pier, for people often dropped small change that rolled through the cracks in the planking and fell to the sands. Halfpence and pennies, sixpences (two and a half new pence) and occasionally shillings (5p) were to be had and once a boy found half-a-crown. (thirty seven and a half p). That was real money, about one sixteenth of many a man's weekly wage.

On return to the shop a penny would be given for each lemonade or mineral water bottle, an enlightened policy that meant few glass bottles were discarded. But this did not seem to work on the beach. People often left them. So the South Beach was divided into gang areas. Ours was from the popular Children's Corner to the first concrete ramp leading down to the beach, and several times during the day we would run a bottle patrol. It brought in anything from threepence to a shilling (twelve bottles), according to the weather, and the satisfaction of knowing that we were clearing away dangerous glass bottles at the same time. It was not all Filthy Lucre.

Tidal Wave

'You should not be making sand castles so close to the steps,' said the red faced man with no neck. He had a greying moustache that curled up at each end and a mouth that went severely down at each end. 'There's plenty of sand nearer the water. Go and play there.'

'We're not building a castle. It's a wall to protect us when the tide comes in, Sir. It's a Spring tide today, extra high, and the sea will come right up to the steps.'

Billy's mother was a lady who stood up for her family. 'Why should they go somewhere else? It's a free beach and they can dig where they like just as you sit where you like. If you choose to sit in the Children's Corner, then you must put up with the little ones.'

The Corner was at the beginning of the South Beach, next to the South Pier, and it was backed by a high curved wall that made it a sun trap and offered protection from the wind. It continued up to the first concrete ramp leading down to the sands, where the Punch and Judy show took place every morning and afternoon. Protection from the sea was given by a long wooden groyne that meant that the water was usually calm, and the rectangular red and white boats, propelled by circular oars, were able to sail in safety. Billy and his friends had been on the boats only once since they cost sixpence a time. The lack of money also meant that they had travelled in a pony cart only once, and that was a year ago. The carts stood near the entrance to the South Pier, between the statue of Neptune and the War Memorial and it was every child's ambition to be taken in the one made up like a small lifeboat. It was proudly decorated in the blue and red of the Royal National Lifeboat Institution and seated about four children, one for each wheel. As the pony trotted you home, the boat swung up and down, in tiny imitation of the mountainous seas often braved by the real lifeboat crew. It felt glorious to wave to your friends trudging home because they had not been so lucky.

Despite these attractions, the little gang thought sand walls built against the sea were much more exciting, and looked forward to the days when the tables showed high water in the afternoon. Today was special. Redface kept complaining.

'Those big shovels you have are a nuisance to us because you are spraying sand all over the place with them. You should have small spades like other children. Look at this sandwich. It cannot be eaten because it is covered in sand.'

'What does he expect on a beach,' muttered Roy. 'Salad cream?'

'Madam, I must insist you keep your children in proper order so that they do not give offence,' continued Redface.

'And I must insist you stop complaining,' replied Billy's Mum. 'They're only doing what children do, playing in the sand. Why don't you go to the North beach and make us all happy? Anyway, we shall all have to leave soon. The waves are getting nearer.'

It was true. Water lapped against the outer wall and in some places it was breaking, so much so that the boys abandoned it and concentrated on strengthening the inner bastion. Like Canute, they knew well the power of the sea and that it would soon pour in, irresistible. Billy sped round the groups of grown ups and whispered, and they made their way up the double flight of wide wooden steps to the sea wall until only Redface and his equally grumpy wife were left.

'Where is everybody proceeding?' he asked.

'Perhaps they'll be back in a minute or two with a jug of tea,' said Billy quickly, shovelling sand into a weak spot. Roy, Johnny and the others were also working hard.

'Wait for it,' said Billy quietly. 'Wait for the big one.'

Then Roy spotted it. 'There,' he hissed. 'Half way from the groyne. A freak, two feet high.'

They all worked furiously, now weakening the wall at its base until the wave struck. The six foot middle section collapsed, and within seconds there was two feet of water below the steps. Mrs Redface yelled and clutched at her handbag that was about to disappear, while her husband grabbed at his hat, floating out to sea through the gap. Johnny lunged for the picnic basket.

'Got it, Sir,' he bawled as he dropped it, causing spoons and knives, cups and plates, to spill out and mingle with the tomato sandwiches, bobbing about like miniature life rafts before they too disappeared beneath the waves.

Helped by the boys and adults who came down the steps to the dry platform, Mr and Mrs Redface, soaked through, scrambled to the promenade.

'You children should be ashamed of yourselves' they spluttered.

'Couldn't be helped, Sir,' said Billy. 'It was a tidal wave.'

Clean Clothes

There was no sharp crack. The tree trunk that had looked so strong slowly and silently collapsed into the ten feet wide drainage ditch that eventually led to the Waveney. Johnny, last across, lost his balance and fell in. He had a great affinity for water and would manage immersion if possible. Venturing on uncertain ice, a rope was always tied round the waist of the one who tested it, but Johnny was never allowed this privilege. He alone would contrive to break through four inches of ice on the Common into a foot of water when nobody else fell in. That was why he was last across.

We all knew that if liggers were going to collapse, it would happen when Johnny, by no means the heaviest of the gang, was coming over. Nobody worried, for he was a good swimmer and it was easy for him to grab the sticks we held out. In less than a minute he was hauled ashore, drenched to the skin and covered in mud, bits of greenery and assorted small creatures, surprised to find themselves in air instead of water.

The countryside was our great outdoor adventure playground, full of rambling hedges, trees and undergrowth, unkempt ditches, ponds and meandering streams. There were tunnel green lanes, dark and mysterious, where the hazel bushes met overhead and the only glimpse of the wide East Anglian sky was at the far end. We could climb, fish, hunt and pick the wild fruit and nuts, all for free, and without interference from grown ups. A favourite area was the wild country to the East of the Common and South of the railway and the river. It was not drained or farmed and was criss crossed with ditches and stretches of water. We called it the Cunnafus.

In Spring there was the wonder of five or six speckled eggs in a nest, a number from which we might take one for a collection and move away quickly so as not to frighten the mother bird into desertion. Later there would be the never ending miracle of half a dozen tiny yellow mouths raised in unison because they thought we were Mum or Dad, bringing food. Johnny, ever clumsy, had once accidentally broken a robin's egg. We had been told not to touch a robin's nest, for if it was harmed your hands would shake for evermore.

There was a dreadful silence. Nobody spoke, but we all knew the rhyme, 'Break a robin's egg, break your own leg,' and fully expected that this would inevitably happen to our friend, now under the curse. He was extra careful right up to the Autumn when the doom allegedly ceased. We told him not to ride his bike.

But now he was in real trouble. Panic had not taken him while in the water, but now he saw a painful immediate future.

'Look at my clothes. When my mother see this mess she'll give me a plate of tongue pie and my father'll half kill me with that belt.'

'No he won't,' said Billy. 'He won't see anything wrong. We'll dry your clothes.'

'Don't be so daft,' moaned Johnny. 'The sun will never dry this lot before tea time.' But Billy had other ideas.

'I was thinking of an oven. My mother's been baking and the fire will still be on. Your things can go in the oven and they'll be dry in no time.'

'But what'll your mother say?'

'Don't worry. She won't be there, but if she is she'll help us.'

So the gang trooped off to Billy's home, at the end of the block opposite from Johnny's and four houses away. They tracked the forbidden route through the back hedge so that his wet state would not be noticed. Nobody was in but the door was unlocked as usual. Johnny reluctantly removed all his clothes and sat morosely wrapped in a blanket.

'Suppose your sister come in?'

'Suppose she do. That blanket cover more of you than your clothes ever did.'

Johnny's things were first washed in the white china sink. The water was dark grey.

'All that dirt didn't come out of the dyke,' said Billy. 'We'd better watch out. Don't want them too clean.'

A stroke of genius led to squeezing the water out of the

clothes by putting them through the mangle. Billy tightened the nuts at the top to give full pressure from the wooden rollers.

'There you are. Nearly dry already.'

The fire was going out in the Triplex black iron range but there was still plenty of warmth. Billy stirred up the embers and set the dampers to push slow heat into the oven.

'Don't burn 'em,' said Johnny. 'My father wouldn't half kill me if I went home in a blanket. He'd really kill me. Are you sure it'll work?'

'Course it will.'

And it did. Two hours later, just in time for tea, Johnny arrived home. His mother gazed at him in astonishment and spoke with surprise.

'Whatever's come over you? You've kept your clothes clean for once'.

Mess-merisation

Crash! Plonk plonk! Tinkle. The noises were coming from the open window of Johnny's front room. He was doing his piano practice and giving voice to a fair imitation of unwilling cows being loaded into a lorry. His mother had decided that he was to have weekly lessons and made sure he practised daily. She did not see why she should pay for this cultural uplift unless he was going to do his bit.

'I - don't - want - to - do - it,' he yelled, thumping the ivories each time to give emphasis to his words. 'It's - a - lot - o'- squit. I - hate - it. It's - bor - ing.'

He ran his hands up and down the keys, still shouting and making no attempt at the scales he was supposed to be fingering.

The gang, sitting on the kerb outside his house, were glad that their parents had neither the money nor inclination for such frills. Some of the boys thought the piano was only for girls, but dare not mention it for fear of Johnny's swift temper and hard fists. It was particularly tough for him in Summer when the windows were open and he knew we were waiting. His father entered the room and joined in the shouting.

'Won't be long now,' said Roy. And it wasn't. Johnny yelled back as his father hit him, broke away and jumped out of the window. His mother screamed about her plants which he had flattened, and father appeared at the front door, red faced and belt swinging. By that time we were away, recalling again that given a hundred or so yards start, no adult could catch us. But we also knew that our poor friend would find the punishment waiting on his return and felt grateful for our more reasonable parents.

One thing Johnny had that few of us experienced was regular birthday parties, his mother's influence again. On these occasions his father tolerated us in a sort of armed truce, for though he punished his son severely, he thought we were just as bad and led him astray. The parties always took the same form – plenty of paste sandwiches, bicycle buns (so called because you needed a bicycle to find the currants) and jelly, followed by games – and sudden disaster to bring things to a memorable conclusion.

Sometimes we did not get beyond the food before trouble began, but this time we managed to get to the games. Arthur, Roy, Billy and Johnny were told to leave the room until we were called. We were policed by Johnny's formidable big sister so that we did not peep. Arthur was the first victim and we wondered what could be happening to him, for the house shook with laughter. Roy and Billy came next and then it was Johnny's turn.

His father told him to sit on a chair facing him and commenced a lecture about Mesmer, the famous hypnotist. He explained that he was also a practitioner and that he was about to mesmerise his son. Johnny was to look straight ahead and stay absolutely still. His sister clearly enjoyed pinning his arms behind the chair just to make sure.

'Now, are you ready?' said father. 'Now I'm going to mess-merise you.'

He ran his fingers firmly over his son's face, first on one side and then on the other, and soot marks appeared wherever he touched. Occasionally he dipped his fingers in a tin to replenish the supply and totally covered the boy's skin. Johnny soon gathered he was being made to look a fool and struggled to free himself, but his sister's hold was too strong. When father had finished he held a looking glass in front of him and said,

'There you are, boy, you're mess-merised.'

It was all too much for Johnny and our laughter pushed him over the edge. His temper rose, and with it his strength. Samson like, he broke free, thumped his sister who began to cry, and with great shouts of rage, struggled to get at the soot. His father was too late to stop him and the tin soared high before crashing down on Mr Strowger's Sunday suited shoulder, scattering soot over his cheek, over daughter Joyce and over the table and sideboard. A dirty cloud rose to colonise the room.

Mrs Strowger began to yell about the mess while Mr S. took off his belt and roared round the table trying to corner Johnny. He kept catching up, but his son took a short cut under the table and regained his lead. Mrs S. was knocked over and the remains of the jelly and sandwiches fell on the floor and were trodden in the melee.

'Time to go,' said Billy. Nobody noticed, for the family was engaged on another of its cathartic rows. As we looked back, louder bawling announced that Johnny had been caught and was suffering more beating.

Next day he told us that he would have got away but for his sister, who had tripped him and jumped on him as he came under the table for the third time.

'Just you wait,' he said darkly. 'One day I shall be as big as her. Then she'll get mess-merised.'

Deception

Roy and Billy rushed into the kitchen fighting, rolling on the floor and shouting while Granny scolded and tried to part them.

'Stop that at once,' she cried. 'How dare you fight in my kitchen.'

She grabbed them both by the scruffs of their necks and dragged them into the living room.

'Now, what's it all about? I thought you two were such good friends.'

'This is what it's all about,' yelled Roy, dancing up and down. He took out his red handled knife with the serrated metal blade. 'He's not my friend. I hate him.'

With that he stabbed Billy in the belly. Billy clutched at his body where Roy held the hilt of the weapon, threw up his arms with a groan and collapsed. Granny screamed, knocked Roy out of the way and knelt down over Billy.

'You wicked boy. What have you done? We must call the doctor at once. How could you do such a thing?'

She rushed to the back door and Billy realised they had gone too far. He stood up.

'You don't need the doctor, grandma. I'm alright. I'm not hurt. It was a joke. Show her the knife, Roy.'

'See, the blade goes into the handle as soon as it meets any resistance.'

He pushed the knife into his hand and the cutting edge disappeared.

'No damage,' said Billy.

'There's likely to be some damage when your grandfather gets home. Roy, you clear off. Billy, up to the attic. In all my life I never met such deception.'

The Wrong Arcade

'There's a slot machine in Gorleston. It's gone wrong,' Roy said. 'You hit it and it gives out pennies.' 'Who told you that?' asked sceptical Billy.

'A boy who lives there. He's had two bob (10p) so far. You have to hit it or it doesn't work.'

So the pair set out for Gorleston, carrying bottles of lemonade made from shop crystals, and bread slices filled with Heinz Sandwich Spread. They could not afford the bus fare from the hoard of nine pennies they had scraped together and had no map, so the only sure way to get there would be along the coast. They walked to Belle Vue Park and struck the North beach and sea wall near the swimming pool. When they reached the sand, it was easy, for the tide was out and it made for firm walking among the ribbed patterns left by the sea. 'How far is it?' said Billy. 'About five or six miles. We should do it easy by dinner time.'

The sea was calm and they played at ducks and drakes, shied stones at seagulls foolish enough to come near, and wrote their names in large letters on the wet sand. When hunger attacked they scrambled to the end of a groyne and ate dangerously, with the water rising and falling underneath.

'Can't see Gorleston,' said Billy, standing up and shading his eyes. 'Maybe we should get a wriggle on.' 'Don't matter. We'll make enough to go back on the bus,' answered Roy.

But when they reached the town a suspicious policeman told them it was half past four and they then had trouble finding the Amusements. The machine they wanted was operated by a lever that propelled a steel ball round a vertical spiral track to a hole in the middle.

'Hope it works,' said Billy as he put in a penny, hit the side of the wooden cabinet and pressed the lever. The ball did not reach the centre and nothing happened.

'Here, let me have a go,' said Roy. He banged hard but still there was no response. He swore at the machine and thumped it till it rocked and the owner shouted at them to stop it or they would be thrown out. The pennies dribbled away and still there was no return.

'Last one,' said Billy. The ball took the path of all the others and no coins came out. He sighed. 'We'd better start for home. It's getting late.'

The beach, the scene of bright confident morning, was a different place, for the tide had come in and left large stretches of shingle. It made walking tiring. At Corton Cliffs the sun had gone, leaving stretches of shadow. Their footsteps faltered on the muscle wrenching pebbles.

Billy pulled his hands into the sleeves of his jumper.

'We'll never get home at this rate and it'll be dark soon. There's some steps up the cliff. Let's go up and see if we can find the road. It'll be easier walking.'

They climbed to the top where a large bearded man in shorts and sandals appeared out of the dusk. He waved his arms and shouted in a high pitched voice.

'It's gone nine o'clock. You're late. I shall write down your names and you will appear before the committee in the morning.'

The boys fled towards the steps as he continued to shout, falling down the last few and dashing over the shingle with new, fear-found energy. When it was clear they were not being pursued they fell on the stones, breathing hard.

'What was all that about?' panted Roy.

'Don't know. Good job we got away. Granny says there's some very funny people in the holiday camps and there's rumours about missing children. We shall have to manage on the beach.'

Next afternoon when the soreness of feet had abated, Roy came to Billy's house.

'We wasted our money,' he said. 'I've just seen that boy from Gorleston and he says it was the wrong amusement arcade.'

One For The Road

It was the season for hoops. Not one would be seen on Monday but on Tuesday there would be dozens in the road, as if some juvenile magic telegraph had operated overnight. Boys used hoops made of iron, while wooden ones were for girls, except when the boomerang game was being played. This involved holding a wooden hoop in your hand, raising it in the air and putting on back spin as you threw it. When it landed, the spin would cause it to return to the thrower. The winner was the one who threw furthest and to whom the hoop came back. The gang, however, considered even iron hoops as cissy, and had turned the activity into something infinitely more exciting and dangerous. They had obtained some old lorry tyres from the dump, a prohibited action and therefore delightful. Into one of these Roy wedged himself and was gently pushed off down the hill. The tyre soon picked up speed but when it came to the bend it continued in a straight line and bounced over the bank into a ditch, fortunately without much water in it. As the first one to try, Roy was something of a hero.

After the countryside, our road on the outskirts of the town was our main playground, especially in poorer weather. Perhaps one vehicle an hour would pass with a small increase on market days or for a few hours on Saturdays. Car drivers knew children would be playing on the tarmacadam and slowed down to give them time to stand aside, or to move the piles of coats that served as goal posts.

All the usual games were played in their seasons. Hopscotch, for which lumps of chalk from the fields were used, and skipping, were favoured mainly by girls while fivestones and clappers were common to both sexes. Long ago, clappers were probably made of bone, but ours were of some sort of hard plastic material bought cheaply from a shop. They were black, slightly curved, and placed between two fingers and shaken, produced a satisfying quick fire noise something like tap dancing. Not all pastimes were so innocuous. Tops fell briefly into disfavour when Arthur's brother, in a wild fury of whipping, managed to get one through a window. This cost him a shilling. Chalking and whipping continued as the top fanatics divided the adults into those for and those against. Tip cat was also criticised and the adults tried to get it abolished on the grounds that a six by one inch piece of wood, pointed at each end, was a dangerous thing to have flying through the air. The answer was to suspend the game if grown ups came by. Stilts were not popular with some householders since they said it gave the chance to look over the hedges and into their front rooms. They did not mind treacle tin stilts. Two large size tins had holes bored in opposite sides and strong string was threaded through before being tied in loops. The loops were held in the hands and lifted with feet on them.

'They're only for little kids and girls,' said Roy.

Conkers was the only pastime with a clear reason for its timing and duration. Many were the closely guarded secret methods of producing a champion fruit. Pickling in vinegar and other liquids, drying in the sun or baking in a slow oven were favourites, though there were those who tried coating them with cement and glue. Some believed that the slightly unripe product of the horse chestnut tree was better material for treatment, and it was these people who started the practice of throwing bits of wood into the trees to bring them down. If the tree were near a road or path there would be trouble from adults who objected to missiles falling from the sky. Dad said they would have to get used to far worse than conkers and bits of wood descending on them.

It was always fun to knock on a door, or ring the bell, and run away to a hiding place from which events could be observed, but it was a simple trick and soon palled. Waiting at the door until it opened and asking to speak to 'Mrs Jones', who did not live there, was much more daring since most people knew the children. If known to the householder, the problem was usually solved by asking for a child whom you knew was out.

Neither of these pieces of mischief required the preparation and skill needed for a major development that could take place only at night. It was essential to be sure that all the houses in the block of four were occupied, for if nobody came to the door the plan failed. There was also the possibility that somebody who lived there was outside and might catch you red handed. When satisfied about these conditions, all four knockers were linked with strong string. One of the gang then thumped on the first door with his fist because it annoyed people if the knocker or bell was not used. Someone opened the door, found nobody there, and maybe swore and shouted because he knew the culprits would be listening. Then he would bang the door violently shut. If the string had been correctly tensioned, by this time his neighbour would be out. It was a very lucky evening if all four could be aroused and out at once, when they would bemoan in loud voices the wickedness of the youth of their time just as many adults do today. The length and tightness of the string were crucial and it required persistent practice. When successful it was certainly One for the Road.

Revolution

Most of our games and pastimes were very old and their seasons came round with the inevitability of eternity. But revolution was in the air. When the first reasonably priced roller skates appeared, everybody asked for them for Christmas and suddenly traditional games were forgotten. Only those who could not get mobile continued with the old pastimes, and not openly because it was an admission that you had no skates.

Skates were made of steel, with a leather toe strap and an ankle strap fixed to a raised, curved section that fitted snugly round the heel of shoe or boot. They came in two varieties, fast skates with ball bearings in the wheels and slower, cheaper models without this refinement. Johnny did not realise this when tomboy Gloria said, 'Race you.'

It was rare for a girl to challenge a boy, but if she did, the challenge must be taken up. Billy tried to warn Johnny, but he would not listen.

'Give you a start,' she added, knowing that the offer would be angrily refused. She stood at the end of the road, arms akimbo, and watched him finish a good twenty yards behind. Poor Johnny was mortified to be so easily beaten.

Wheels wore out in a few months and cost tuppence (1p) for non ball bearing and sixpence (two and a half p) for the superior models. These rose to eight pence in 1939 as the war neared and demands on steel ball bearings increased. As we became proficient skaters, football suffered and was replaced by roller hockey and for a time there was a league with three teams. One of these rejoiced in the name of Beverley Hills United. Matches were played in the road with orange boxes for goals and supposedly independent referees who disclaimed any responsibility for the disorder that often occurred on and off the pitch.

The counter revolution was led by marbles, mainly because one of its variants could be played in the gutters on the way to school. The objective of the knock on game was to hit and thus capture your opponent's pieces. It made the journey more acceptable, but players were sometimes so fascinated that they lost count of time and were punished for being late. Since it was forbidden to take skates to school, the gutter game continued and soon the bibby hole game made a come-back too. To score and become the owner of all the marbles in the game you had to be good at getting all your pieces in the hole, although the rules were complicated and three in might cause you to lose. Clay marbles, bought very cheaply, and of different dark colours, were the standard currency and the proud possessors of highly decorated glass marbles often called them alleys and kept them as exhibits. It was rather like men who collected guns but never fired them. Half way products, translucent pop alleys from Codd's bottles, were used in games although screw on and other types of closure had superseded these lemonade bottles. It mattered little to us that the brewers, fearful for their trade, called the non-alcoholic contents 'Coddswallop.'

Roller skating dominated for one season and briefly into the next. Then all the old traditional pastimes came back and skating fitted into the pattern. The revolution was over.

Running The Dinosaur

Two dinosaurs actually. They both lived on the bridge at Lowestoft and were there from the opening of the old swing span in 1897 until its closure in 1969. Grown ups did not notice the creatures, since only their posteriors, about two feet wide, were visible. These parts of their anatomies separated pedestrians from wheeled traffic on either side, and rose in gentle curves from road level at the ends to heights of about two feet in the middle. That was their purpose said the adults, that and the support and strengthening of the bridge. But we knew better. Their backs were topped with four rows of bumps that looked like round head rivets protruding about half an inch. It was not easy to walk on them, let alone run, and of course such activity was strictly prohibited.

The footways guarded by the dinosaurs had other attractions. Juvenile hands could easily be slipped through the diamond shaped metal trellis that stopped people from falling into the water, but it did not prevent the dropping of small missiles on passing boats. Experts could spit through the spaces, but these were random shots that seldom hit anything, while a good stone dropper allowed for the speed of wind and boat and sometimes achieved remarkable accuracy. It was no good climbing the five feet lattice. Adults would interfere and the bridge master would notice. For this reason, all droppings had to be unseen, and practised on the southern end of the bridge on the western or inner harbour side. From there escape was simple.

Running the dinosaur was much more exciting and dangerous. The trick was to mount at the South Pier end, and run across without being caught by the bridge master. It was comparatively easy to avoid capture at times of heavy traffic since he would have to cross the road to reach offenders. Running the eastern, or outer harbour side was much more difficult because his office, with a large window view, was on the same side. Only older boys, wearing soft shoes, and skilled at fast movement over the treacherous bumps of the dinosaur's back had any hope of success. If caught, there would be a fierce ding on the ear, a buffet on the head, or both, and parents might be informed. What else was to be expected if you wished to become a bridge hero and member of the Royal Order of Dinosaur Runners?

Pop Gun

It was called a pop gun because it went pop. But there was a lot of skilled work before that stage was reached.

A good straight piece of elder was required, about six to eight inches long and about one and a half inches in diameter, and it was usually cut from the bush with a saw. Some people said it was unlucky to cut elder because the Cross was made of elder, but others maintained that Judas Iscariot was hanged from a tree of the same wood. It seemed to us that the two superstitions cancelled one another out. They did not prevent us from

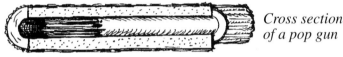

Cross section of a pop gun

moving to the exciting part. Some of the soft pith in the centre could be removed with a hand drill and a stout metal rod, but always, necessary or not, a red hot poker, heated in the coal fire, was used for the finishing touches. Mother insisted that this should be done outside because of the smell and hissing of the pith, from which moisture would often drip. The elder was put into a vice for this operation. When it was clean and straight inside the barrel it was time to make the brush.

Nuttery was best for this. If the barrel of the gun was half an inch wide, then a piece of hazel an inch or more in diameter would be chosen. A spokeshave or knife was used to take it down to half an inch, leaving a block at one end for a handle. The other end was steeped in water and with gentle cuts from a knife was made into a brush, certainly the most difficult and perhaps the most crucial part of the process. When the brush was inserted into the barrel it should be airtight. To test, a finger would be put over the business end and the hazel brush pumped.

The only projectiles used were halved acorns, which explained why this was an autumn pastime. The piece of acorn was pushed in, curved bit first, and then banged home on a flat surface. The brush was inserted at the other end, pushed in gently for about an inch, and then rammed down very quickly. Some people positioned the gun against the stomach, and used both hands to press hard. If the work had been good the result was a satisfying loud pop, a missile flying up to twenty five yards, and an even more satisfying yell from the target of your pop gun.

Big as Footballs

'Where is it then?' asked Johnny.

'Shut your tater trap,' hissed Billy. 'They'll get suspicious.'

Johnny ignored him.

'You said it was as big as footballs and now you can't find it.'

'It's over there, under the pile of straw. They cover it up so people won't be upset.'

The little gang moved towards the yellow pyramid.

'Now, you move the straw, Johnny. You're the one who didn't believe.'

'Like Thomas in the Bible,' put in Arthur.

Johnny began the job.

'Phew. What a pong.'

He took out his snot rag and made it into a mask for his mouth. 'Well thass a rum'un. Just look at them, each one really as big as a football. Do they do several at a time?'

'It must be very painful getting rid of things that size,' said Arthur. 'My Mum gives me senna pods or Empire Californian Syrup of Figs.'

'Depends on the size of the hole you fool,' muttered Johnny, busily engaged in clearing all the straw away, and inevitably getting his hands truly plastered with the olive coloured mess. Billy knew it would be his clothes next.

'You needn't go any further,' he said. 'Wipe your hands on the grass and then rinse them under that tap.'

What they had uncovered was a heap of elephant droppings, discreetly relegated to a corner of the Blackboy meadow, away from the Big Top. The circus had been in the town for a couple of days and would move on after the Saturday performance, to return next year. Although small, it had a good range of wild animals and boasted a band, clowns, horses, dogs, and a fire eater.

'Why not come tonight?' proposed Johnny. 'We could get in under the canvas.'

'Won't work,' said Billy. 'They know about that trick. The Town gang tried it last year and they clipped their ears and made them load the elephant muck. Better to find sixpence from somewhere and come to the matinee tomorrow afternoon.'

'Why not sell the elephant muck?' said Arthur. 'We sell horse muck.'

'And how do we get it home, stupid?' said Johnny. 'And who's going to buy it? Probably kill all your plants. And what are they going to be doing while we steal their muck?'

The much envied circus children came to school for the few days. After hearing about their lives, many a boy secretly resolved to run away with the circus, especially after the performance of the scantily clad young ladies on the trapeze. The fair, twice yearly, had the same effect.

It was Bert Stocks' fair on the meadow during late Autumn, memorable because of the horse that had died while the fair was there. It had fallen on the slippery road and the gang watched, listening to its heavy breathing that gradually declined till it stopped for ever. All four were late for school that morning and were unusually quiet. If horses could die, so could human beings.

They all managed one go on the dodgems, but after that the only person who had any money left was Roy.

'I'm going on the coconuts,' he said. He was the best shot they had and fancied his chances. 'They look like human heads but are full of sweet white water.'

'They're not real coconuts,' warned Billy. 'They're made up to look real and are set in sawdust. It's hard to knock them off.'

Roy paid threepence for three balls, the children's rate, and was allowed to stand three feet in front of the adult line. His first shot thudded against the canvas backing, but the next two were dead on target. The coconut that was not a coconut quivered and rocked, but did not fall.

'Well done, my boy,' shouted the showman. 'Have another go.'

His first shot hit the target but the nut did not drop. Nor did it fall when he hit it twice more.

'They're stuck on,' shouted Billy to the restive crowd, but the stall holder saw what was coming.

'They're not stuck on,' he said, lifting one up. 'You're a good shot, boy, but not strong enough as yet to knock them off. Here, have a coconut.'

Roy was pleased.

'Not as big as a football,' he said. 'But better to carry home than elephant droppings.'

Always a Way

'I wish I could have a go with that hose,' said Billy. 'I could just do with cooling down.'

The little gang watched from the market fence as Penny cleaned the car. Water splashed and thudded against the metal work and gurgled off the vehicle in fountains as he swept gallons along the bonnet and over the roof. When the telephone rang he turned off the tap and moved inside the garage.

'Come on, then. Now's our chance.'

'He'll come out again,' said Arthur. 'Suppose it's a short call.'

'Alright, scaredy cat. You stay here and keep watch. Shout loud if he come.'

Roy and Billy scampered over the road, turned on the tap and began to squirt water. First they deluged the car. Then it was the children coming down the lane from school who suffered and ran screaming and shouting, yet secretly glad to have a wetting on such a hot Summer day. As with all pranks, it developed, and cars received jets through their open windows, yet none stopped. Finally it was the passers by who received the full force when Billy took over. Everybody ran, fearing that if they tried to stop the boys they would get even wetter. It was fascinating work till Arthur shouted a warning. Roy ran immediately but Billy turned to find Penny upon him. Vainly did he soak him from head to toe, hoping that he would give up as the other adults had done. But the owner was made of sterner stuff.

'You young devil,' he bawled. 'I'll box your ears.'

Billy dropped the water pipe and turned to run but it was too late. Penny grabbed him under one arm, picked up the hose, now writhing like a snake, and turned it off. Billy yelled and fought. He managed to break free, kicking Penny on the shin. But the portly garage owner was surprisingly swift for a large man and grabbed him again. Now that he had two hands he held the boy firmly and banged him about the head and ears.

'Now then, boy, what's your name?'

'Shan't tell.'

Penny dinged him on both ears.

'Ow. That hurt.'

'It was meant to hurt. There's another. Now do you tell me your name.'

'Shan't. I'll tell my father.'

'I'll tell your father when I've got your name.'

Billy was silent.

'Alright then. You can stay in the office till you come to your senses and tell me who you are.'

He dragged the struggling boy inside, pushed him into a corner, thrust a few papers into a drawer and locked it.

'Now, do you stay here till you give me your name and address.'

'Shan't. Not ever.'

Penny locked the door and disappeared. Billy turned the handle quietly but the lock was firm. He examined the window. The panes of glass were too small to get through, so smashing one would not help. Standing on the sloping desk he was able to reach the ceiling but it was hard, and any noise would bring Penny back to investigate. He had been brought up to believe there was always a way, but there seemed no way this time. He sat in a corner, supported by the two walls, and not visible from the window. Penny passed by, paused and dashed to unlock the door.

'What are you doing down there?'

'More comfortable.'

'Do you tell me your name and address you can go home.'

Billy was silent and he locked the door. Fifteen minutes later he came again, then at decreasing intervals. Always he demanded, 'Tell me your name.'

'It's not Jacob,' said Billy, referring to the Bible hero's wrestling match with the angel, but Penny was unmoved. After several visits Billy said, 'It's half past five. My father works at the Shell Mex. He'll be home just after six. If I'm not there, he'll call the police. You'll be in trouble then.'

He could tell Penny was worried.

'I shan't tell if you let me go.'

'Alright then. But if you play with my hose again, I'll call the police myself and your father will have to pay for the damage.'

Penny dinged his ears once more, pushed him out of the office and tried to trip him up as he ran off.

It was quiet outside. A low voice hissed from the trees near the fence. It was Roy. He dropped to the ground.

'You alright? What did he do?'

'Dinged my ears and wanted my name.'

'Did you tell him?'

'No. I knew he couldn't keep me there much longer. There's always a way.'

The Reason Why

Many times in our young lives did gambling lead down to ruin, laziness to poverty and stealing to prison. In the other direction, kindness brought reward, punctuality blossomed into advancement and honesty made for success. These were the lessons of the snakes and ladders board game that my grandmother bought me in 1930 from a toy shop in Lowestoft. It was the same establishment from which she was later to comfort me after my first visit to the dentist 'up a' Kirkley', as she called the area beyond what was then the Grand cinema. At that time it was the first lead animals of my farmyard that she purchased, black and white Friesian cows, massive looking Suffolk Punch horses and pink pigs, surrounded by their lovable sucklings. Years later, when I had grown out of toy animals, her wrath was incurred when I swapped the whole collection for a four wheeled go-cart.

Neither the quality bone dice nor handsome wooden shaker survived the wear and tear of three generations, but the board itself, now framed and covered in plastic, continues to give out the moral precepts of the Protestant ethic by which we lived. It still comes down from the wall to continue its stern messages.

The children who have had so much fun from this simple game have often doubted, as they grew older, the truth of some of the pictures. At square 21, labelled Industry, a miner is shown toiling underground with his pick, while the ladder runs upward to Prosperity at 82. Here he is well clothed and fed, gazing proudly out of his office window at the three chimneys of his own factory. Presumably he earned so much by his Industry in the pit that he was able to change his occupation. This was clearly the most important idea to come across since it gave an increase of 61 squares. Obedience at square 8, leading upward to Respect at 26 was insignificant beside the miner's success.

The snakes, of course, had been causing trouble since one of them had Adam and Eve expelled from the Garden of Eden. They were nauseating creatures, and to land on one was to receive greater penalties than the ladders gave success, teaching us, I suppose, that life was tough and that you should not get into evil ways. Bad Temper at 98, only two from home, and showing the culprit attacking a man, swiftly resulted in Murder at 13, the biggest move on the board with 85 squares to descend and a horrific picture of the murderer and his victim at the end. Was this the reason why, I wondered, that I often warned my sons and their sons against the folly of losing your temper?

The Ten Shilling Note

Snakes and ladders was our favourite, but we played other board and dice games like Ludo, where there was always an argument about strategy. Some people believed it was best to keep as many of your four pieces as possible in play at the same time so that advantage could be taken of whatever the dice gave. More cautious spirits were all for getting one piece home before bringing out another. Draughts took our fancy occasionally but Chess, like Halma, never caught on. We invented our own game with the Halma men. They stood, two by two, on dominoes and were carried over the sea of the board, to shipwreck and drowning or to the safety of the harbour, according to the throw of the dice and the skill shown in using the numbers given. Perhaps in this was the influence of the lifeboat and our grandfather, lost on the Brixham smack Conqueror before we were born. Blow football and Tiddly Winks were popular but the dart board so beloved of Dad and his friends held no interest.

Commercial pressures were beginning to show. We used Gibbs Solid Dentrifice, a cheap individual circular pink cake on which you scrubbed your wet toothbrush, and played the game that came free when sufficient tokens had been collected. A winding track, filled with hazards like too many sweets and lack of proper dental care, led eventually to the shining tooth castle. There you were free at last from the attentions of Giant Decay. He stalked the way and threatened caries or worse at every bend, reminding us of Giant Despair in The Pilgrim's Progress.

Clockwork toys were more expensive, but Christmas and birthday presents, along with second hand purchases and swapping less attractive toys, gave us a Hornby set. It had two of the cheapest engines, an oval of gauge 'O' track and two points. There was neither inclination nor money for stations and signals. One person was in charge of each point, while others controlled the locomotives. The objective was to avoid collisions but it often seemed that violent rail crashes were the real aim. Savings once allowed us to buy a more sophisticated engine that had a reverse lever, and this did sterling duty for several years until fashions changed to aerial railways. The casing came off the apple green London and North Eastern Railway 0-4-0 tank engine, Dad did some soldering, and cardboard coaches were hauled on lines of string from kitchen to living room. In a final incarnation, the engine had metal blades attached and became the heart of a paddle steamer, a last tribute to the quality and durability of Hornby clockwork.

As the war came nearer there was more money about and we could buy sixpenny (two and a half new pence) clockwork cars modelled on the £100 Ford Popular. They had removable rubber tyres and were raced along tracks bounded by walls made from a second hand Meccano set, another

of our favourites. It seems to me now a much more versatile, imaginative and demanding toy than its plastic successors where pieces are clipped on. There were nuts and bolts to screw together. We saw ourselves as engineers who would go abroad to the Empire to service steam locomotives and other products of the home factories. Further intimations of the war to come were in the anti aircraft guns that shot matchsticks, though they failed to stop the tanks with rubber caterpillar tracks that started again if they were knocked over. Ominously, perhaps, from Germany came the Shuco car that could be guided with a hand steering wheel attached to the vehicle with a long wire. It was fascinating to stand up and zig-zag it through a line of small posts.

Also fascinating, and taking up a lot of our time, were the many comics available. Chick's Own, printed on good quality paper, was for the very youngest and long words were hy-phen-ated to make it easier to read. Older children sneered at it, so everybody's ambition was to get onto Chips, Radio Fun, and other simple comic strips, all made from poor paper in different colours and low prices (one halfpenny, which is four comics for 1p). At the peak were magazine type booklets like Wizard, Hotspur, Triumph, Champion and Magnet, that cost two pence (1p). They printed cliff hanging stories rather than picture strips. All titles were eagerly awaited and swapped until they fell to pieces. Most adults, while doing nothing about the lack of books for children, looked down their noses at comics, yet they inadvertently formed an effective rudimentary reading scheme. Many children wanted to learn, and were prepared to work at the business of reading in order to keep up with their comic wise peers. If you could not discuss the latest exploits of the Scarlet Speedster you really were out in the cold.

Monopoly came in with a bang and all other pastimes, inside or out, were forgotten. One of our better off friends received a set as a present and we spent most of our time round his house immersed in the greedy intricacies of the property market. It was like a drug. This was clear from Peter's behaviour in the middle of a game, since he pulled out what he thought was a chocolate wrapping and threw it on the fire. As it flared we stared in horror. It was a ten shilling note. It took my father a day to earn as much.

Other East Anglian titles
available from

THE HOBBIES STORY
Terry Davy
Over 100 years of the history of a well known fretwork and engineering company

MEMORIES OF NORFOLK CRICKET
Philip Yaxley
200 years of history of Norfolk Cricket

LARN YARSELF NORFOLK
Keith Skipper
A comprehensive guide to the Norfolk dialect

RUSTIC REVELS
Keith Skipper
Humorous country tales and cartoons

LARN YARSELF SILLY SUFFOLK
David Woodward
A comprehensive guide to the Suffolk dialect

TATTERLEGS FOR TEA
David Woodward
More Suffolk Dialect in Yarns and Verse

MIGHTA BIN WUSS
Tony Clarke
Tales of Ow Jimma

LARN YERSALF NORTHAMPTONSHIRE
Mia Butler and Colin Eaton
A comprehensive guide to the Northamptonshire dialect